TRANSLATIONS FROM GREEK AND ROMAN AUTHORS

Series Editor: GRAHAM TINGAY

PLAUTUS

Rudens · Curculio · Casina

Translated by CHRISTOPHER STACE

CAMBRIDGE UNIVERSITY PRESS

Cambridge
London   New York   New Rochelle
Melbourne   Sydney

Published by the Press Syndicate of the University of Cambridge
The Pitt Building, Trumpington Street, Cambridge CB2 1RP
32 East 57th Street, New York, NY 10022, USA
296 Beaconsfield Parade, Middle Park, Melbourne 3206, Australia

First published 1981

Printed in Great Britain by
REDWOOD BURN LIMITED
Trowbridge, Wiltshire

Library of Congress catalogue card number: 81–6086

British Library Cataloguing in Publication Data
Plautus, Titus Maccius
Rudens; Curculio; Casina. – (Translations from
Greek and Roman authors)
I. Title   II. Plautus, Titus Maccius. Curculio
III. Plautus, Titus Maccius. Casina
IV. Stace, Christopher   V. Series
872'.01   PA6570

ISBN 0 521 28046 X

Permission to perform Christopher Stace's translations
of Plautus's *Rudens, Curculio* and *Casina* should be
        from Deborah Rogers Ltd., 5–11 Mortimer Street, London W.1.

The cover picture is from a wall painting in the Casa di Casca
in Pompeii, showing a scene from a Roman comedy, in which an
old slave mocks two ladies. It is reproduced by courtesy of the Mansell Collection.

Contents

INTRODUCTION

Roman Comedy

When we speak of Roman Comedy, we are referring, in the main, to the works of two famous comic playwrights, Plautus and Terence. Plautus (his dates are usually given as 254–184 B.C.), was the earlier, more prolific and successful of the two. He came from Sarsina in Umbria, and his full name was Titus Macc(i)us Plautus. The details of his life are obscure, but he is thought to have been in the theatrical profession, perhaps as an actor-manager. His surviving plays show great theatrical skill and knowledge of stagecraft. Twenty of his plays still exist in more or less complete form, as well as many fragments, and we know this represents only part of his output. Terence (Publius Terentius Afer, died *c.* 160 B.C.) may have come from Africa as a slave, and taken the name of the man who set him free. His total output was six comedies, and we have them all intact; but he was nothing like as popular as Plautus.

The comedies these two (and other playwrights like them) wrote are called *fabulae palliatae* – i.e. plays in Greek dress – and were adaptations from the Greek New Comedies produced some 50 to 100 years earlier. It was only natural, when Rome turned to comedy, that she should be inclined to take over the already rich and fully developed comic tradition of her neighbours, the Greeks. So, to understand Roman Comedy, it is necessary to understand something of the nature of Greek Comedy, whose plots and form it borrowed.

The Greeks had passed from the 'Old' Comedy of Aristophanes (mid fifth century – *c.* 380 B.C.), with its fantastic plots, political satire, and formal choral interludes, through the so-called 'Middle' Comedy (from *c.* 400 B.C. on), a transitional phase, to the New Comedy (from *c.* 336 B.C. on), whose most brilliant exponent was Menander (*c.* 342–292 B.C.). Menander wrote about a hundred plays, of which only a few survive in tolerable completeness, though there are many fragments. Some of the characteristics of the New Comedy are the development of complicated plots, the portrayal of subtle character, and the introduction of romantic love as a theme. However, the chorus of Old Comedy disappeared, and its place was taken by musicians who provided musical interludes, and accompanied the lyrical passages, but who were extraneous to the action of the play. The characters were predominantly middle class, and the comedy might be called a social 'comedy of manners'. The New Comedy was more like some of the melo-dramas of Euripides, the youngest of the three great Attic Tra-gedians, than the Old Comedy of Aristophanes. Menander was highly regarded in antiquity, and, through the medium of Roman Comedy, he has exercised a considerable influence on more modern comedy. Molière, Sheridan and Congreve, for example, were among his many imitators. Another great writer of New Comedy was Diphilus of Sinope, on whose originals Plautus based both his *Rudens* and *Casina*, which are included in this translation.

What exactly Plautus did when he 'adapted' the Greek originals (and indeed how he got hold of the scripts in the first place) has been long disputed. However, with the acquisition of increasing numbers of papyri over the last three-quarters of a century, and at last the discovery of part of the original play by Menander on which Plautus based his *Bacchides*, we can now see that this 'adap-tation' was far more than mere translation. So far as one can judge, Plautus imported the basic structure of the plot (though in *Casina*, for example, he truncates it ruthlessly), the Greek costumes and characters, but he freely introduces elements from Roman life when he thinks fit. The result, as the reader soon sees, is a complete fusion of these disparate elements. Some of the jokes, the names, the customs referred to, are purely Roman, and would have meant little or nothing to a Greek audience. Similarly, jokes which would have been obscure or unintelligible to a Roman audience, Plautus would have suppressed; situations which suggested comic possibil-ities to him, would have been freely expanded. Topical allusions, too, are occasionally inserted. The French comedian Molière main-tained that 'the sole aim of comedy is to please', and in Plautus we have a playwright who saw the theatrical truth of this more clearly than most. The plot is merely his framework; but wit and farce and laughter, whatever the method used to achieve them, are more im-portant. Plautus knew how to keep his audience amused: puns play an important part in his comic armoury; certain comic motifs recur (for example: mistaken identity; the brilliantly resourceful slave contrasted with a dim master; dashing entries, and angry, blustering exits); indecencies were frequent and Roman audiences never tired of them; new word-coinages, fantastic and humorous made-up names, can have great comic value; violation of the dramatic illusion (see the end of *Casina*), then, as now, could produce a startling effect, and always seems to amuse an audience ('This is only a play, after all!').

In comparison with Plautus, Terence is more sedate, more subtle, less farcical – and, significantly, was less popular at Rome. His most successful attempt was *Eunuchus* ('The Eunuch'), his most farcical and 'Plautine' comedy. Above all, Plautus understood how to satisfy the needs of his audiences, and in doing so showed great comic inventiveness and ingenuity. His plays have immense gusto, and can move at a breathless pace. The list of those who have been influenced by him is very long: Shakespeare and Jonson are obvious examples.

In the Old Comedy, the Chorus had played a full and important part, but by the time New Comedy was flourishing, the role of the Chorus was minimal and incidental to the action, being reduced merely to a musical interlude designed to break up the action and account for lapses of time off-stage. Plautus dispensed altogether with the choral element; his plays were written for continuous performance (the act divisions that commonly appear in editions of Plautus originated sometime during the fifteenth century), and the stage is rarely empty. From time to time the audience has to assume a lapse of time off-stage, but this is usually obvious. In *Curculio*, in order to solve this 'problem' and bridge the gap, Plautus ingeniously brings on the Stage Property Manager to amuse the audience!

The plays of Plautus and Terence, like all other surviving dramas of Greece and Rome, are in verse. The metre of conversation and monologue is generally iambic (as in Shakespeare's 'If músic bé the fóod of lóve, play ón!'), sometimes trochaic (a favourite rhythm was that of 'Iń the spríng a yóung man's fáncy líghtly túrns to thóughts of lóve'). Plautus also composed lyrics (*cantica*, set-pieces in a variety of metres) which would have been sung, though presumably not quite in the manner of operatic arias; perhaps they were given a variety of treatments, depending on the degree of emotion necessary. The longer metres were chanted, and both they and the lyrics had a musical accompaniment. This would have been of a primitive nature, and probably amounted to no more than a single wind instrument, commonly called a 'flute', but more accurately a 'pipe', with a reed in the mouthpiece. The preponderance of lyrics in Plautus (in *Casina*, for example, nearer a half than a third of the play is composed in lyrics) is an important innovation, and in this respect at least he seems closer to Old Comedy than New. It is a significant aspect of his *variety*, and a close examination of his plays reveals a conscious and skilful attempt to alternate monologue, dialogue and song. It is hard to think of a modern equivalent to this Plautine mixture of song and spoken verse – perhaps it could be compared to a rather racy version of Gilbert and Sullivan's style of operetta.

Roman society in Plautus's plays

It is necessary now to say something about the society described in these plays, as at first glance, to the twentieth-century reader, it may appear both immoral and decadent. The society we meet in the plays of Plautus is, with certain modifications, that of the Greek dramatist Menander, whose plays he was adapting. The people Menander wrote about were upper-middle-class, and so far as they were concerned the two purposes of marriage were to produce freeborn children, and to preserve family property. As happens in such societies, marriages were arranged, and love had no place in the preliminaries. If a young man looked for romantic love of the sort regarded as normal today, he had to turn elsewhere, to professional 'companions', called *hetaerae* (freeborn, non-Athenian and independent), *pallacae* (also freeborn and foreign, but usually kept by their patrons), and, at the bottom of the scale, *pornae* or prostitutes. The *pornae* were slaves, and owned by a pimp, who would often have them taught to dance and to play a musical instrument so that he could make money out of them by hiring them out to entertain at parties. Whatever his companion was, the young man needed money. If the girl was a *hetaera*, he would need to buy her presents as tokens of his love; if a mere *porne*, she had to be paid for, and, if he loved her, he needed to find money to purchase her freedom. Most of the plays are concerned with the plight of a money-less young man in love with such a girl (Plautus is not worried about assigning her to her correct category, and indeed in the Roman world such subtle distinctions did not exist) and the tricks of his slave (in *Curculio* the parasite) to secure her freedom. In a common variation of this theme, the *porne* turns out to be free (*Rudens*, *Casina*) and of Athenian birth, so that she can, after all, marry the young man who loves her. Often, most conveniently, she proves to be the long-lost daughter of the next door neighbour, and, to our great satisfaction, they are happily reunited. Touchingly, the *porne* has been merely a probationer, or, if she is pregnant, it proves to be because of an anonymous assault by someone who turns out to be none other than her intended husband. So all's well that ends well, and, seen in this light, Plautus's plays can hardly be said to be either immoral or distasteful.

Performance and staging

In Plautus's day, these plays were performed at various festivals, or *Ludi*, in the Roman calendar, which occurred in April, May, July, September and November. They were put on in the open air by professional companies on a temporary wooden stage (there was no permanent stone theatre at Rome until Pompey built one in 55 B.C.); this 'stage' was about 1½ metres high, and may have been as much as 55 metres long. (If it was this long, the conventions of soliloquies, asides, eavesdropping, and failure to see other characters arriving, may not have appeared as unnatural to the ancient audience as they do to the modern reader.) In most plays the stage represented a city street in Athens, and behind it was a stage-building, a background painted to resemble the front of one, two or three houses, behind which the actors could change costume, and so on. There may also have been a temple-entrance (as in *Curculio*), or an altar, as the play required. Actors could enter the stage not only through the doorways but also by either wing, and it is a convention in Roman Comedy that Stage Left was the entrance from the Forum and City, and Stage Right that from the Harbour and Abroad. *Rudens* is untypical in many respects: its setting is unique – the sea-coast, with one cottage only on stage, and a temple of Venus in the background – and the City and Harbour are located on the same side of the stage.

Admission to plays was free, and the audience was drawn from both sexes and all social classes. The conditions must have been rather like those of the Elizabethan theatre – noisy, informal, and cheerfully philistine! Often in the prologue the author has to ask the audience for its attention, and we know that one play of

INTRODUCTION

Terence's was a flop at its first performance because the audience turned its attention to the rival attraction of a tight-rope walker, or some boxers – and the second time it was performed the audience suddenly vanished when there were rumours of a gladiatorial exhibition!

Costumes were modelled on those of the Greek New Comedy (*palliatae* = 'played in the Greek *palla*'), i.e. the usual dress of ordinary Greek citizens, and slaves. The basic piece of clothing was the tunic, a shirt with holes for the neck and arms. This was covered by an over-garment, long in the case of free citizens, short for slaves, soldiers, and sometimes also young men; cooks wore a short tunic belted at the waist. Different characters wore different colours; apparently prostitutes wore yellow. The women (wives *and* prostitutes) wore long, flowing over-garments. The normal footwear was a thin sandal or slipper. Wigs would be of different colours to underline the different roles: usually white for an old man, black for a young man, red for a slave – but no doubt these distinctions were not rigid. The question of whether or not the actors wore masks is still hotly debated. In Greek drama there had originally been only three actors, who doubled roles, and were assisted by mute 'supers'; in Roman Comedy, so far as we know, there were no such restrictions. Many of the plays require at least five speaking parts, but doubtless economy imposed restrictions of its own. What is clear is that, if the actors of Roman Comedy wore masks, the doubling of roles and playing of 'twin' parts (as in *Amphitruo* and *Menaechmi*) would have been made much easier. But scholars cannot agree about the matter: the evidence is inconclusive, and we must leave the case for masks unproven.

For those interested in pursuing the subject of Roman Comedy beyond the confines of this brief introduction, the list of books below will be helpful.

Suggested reading

Arnott, W.G., *Menander, Plautus and Terence*, Greece and Rome: New Surveys in the Classics (Oxford, Clarendon Press, 1975)

Beare, W., *The Roman Stage* (Methuen, third edition 1969)

Bieber, M., *The History of the Greek and Roman Theater* (Princeton University Press, second edition 1961)

INTRODUCTION

Duckworth, G.E., *The Nature of Roman Comedy* (Princeton University Press, 1952)

Sandbach, F.H., *The Comic Theatre of Greece and Rome* (Chatto and Windus, 1977)

Note: the small raised numbers which occur in the texts of the plays e.g. time[1] indicate a note of explanation to be found at the end of that play.

Rudens

The *Rudens*, considered by many to be Plautus's masterpiece, was adapted from a play (possibly *Epitrope*, 'The Arbitration', or *Pera*, 'The Wallet') by the Greek comic playwright Diphilus. Untypically, the play is not set in a street in Athens, but in Cyrene, a Greek colony on the coast of North Africa. On stage stands the Temple of Venus, and the cottage of an old Athenian expatriate, Daemones.

Daemones' daughter Palaestra, stolen from him in her childhood, has fallen into the hands of Labrax, a rascally pimp, who brings her to Cyrene. A young Cyrenean, Plesidippus (who is by birth, as it turns out, Athenian), has fallen in love with her, and, intending to purchase her from Labrax, gives him a part-payment. But the pimp tries to make off to Sicily with both Palaestra *and* the money. A storm (sent by Arcturus, the stellar divinity who speaks the prologue) wrecks his ship, and the pimp and the girl are cast ashore. A fisherman hauls up the trunk containing Labrax's valuables, and among them in a box are some trinkets of Palaestra's, which finally prove that she is the long-lost daughter of old Daemones.

This is therefore a recognition play, although the action is largely concerned with the efforts of Labrax to make off with his 'slavegirl', and those of Daemones and others to stop him. The climax comes when Palaestra is found to be freeborn, and Daemones' daughter; the play can thus end happily with the promise of a wedding.

'*Rudens*' is usually taken to mean 'rope' – evidently the rope by which Gripus the fisherman drags up his strange 'catch' – the trunk belonging to Labrax. The 'tug-of-war' scene (lines 1369 ff.) between Gripus and Plesidippus's slave Trachalio is central to the play, and perhaps its most lively and amusing episode.

The unusual out-of-doors setting (compare Shakespeare's *The Tempest*, which has more than one parallel with *Rudens*), the romantic interest, and the relatively high moral tone of this play make it unique in Plautus. Gripus's general surliness and determination to hang on to his catch (his 'trunkfish'), and the unashamed, genial crookedness of the pimp Labrax, are memorable features in a play which is rich both in character and dramatic incident. Note the serious treatment of the two shipwrecked girls' plight (where lyrics increase the note of pathos), which provides an excellent foil for the comic scenes.

Rudens

CHARACTERS

Arcturus	Stellar divinity who speaks the prologue
Daemones	Elderly Athenian expatriate living in the cottage on stage
Sceparnio	His slave
Gripus	Another of his slaves, a fisherman
Palaestra	Daughter of Daemones, who was kidnapped by pirates and sold to a pimp many years ago
Ampelisca	Her friend in misfortune
Plesidippus	A young man of Cyrene, also Athenian by birth
Trachalio	His slave
Labrax	A pimp
Charmides	His friend
Ptolemocratia	Old priestess of the shrine of Venus
Turbalio } **Sparax**	Two other slaves of Daemones
Fishermen	
Plesidippus's friends	

The hour is just before dawn. Arcturus, the brightest star in the constellation Boötes, comes on as the Prologue.

Arcturus   I come from the Celestial Commonwealth above, a fellow-citizen of Him who sways all peoples, and all seas and lands. I am, as you see, a brightly shining star, a constellation which always rises at the appointed time[1] here on earth and in heaven. By night I shine brightly in the sky and have the gods for company; by day I walk in disguise among mortal men, as other constellations do, falling from heaven to earth.

    For Jupiter, Lord of Gods and Men, assigns each

of us our different places among the peoples, so that we can assess the characters of men, watch what they do, their ways, their deeds of piety and decency, so that He may reward each man with his proper portion of prosperity.   15

If there are any who try to bend the law by producing false witnesses, or who deny their debts on oath, we note their names and take the list to Jove. Each and every day He knows exactly who's heading for trouble. If wicked men here think they can win their lawsuits by perjuring themselves, or make crooked claims before a judge, He just reopens the case – and judges the whole thing again! And the fine He makes them pay makes what they've gained falsely look *trifling*!

Of course, he has the names of all decent men written down on a different set of tablets.

The crooked actually think they can placate Jove with gifts and sacrifices – but they are actually wasting their time and money. This is because He never listens to the prayer of a perjurer; the righteous man's prayers will always win the god's pardon more easily than the sinner's will. So I warn you, all of you who lead pious and upright lives: just continue that way, and one day you'll be glad that you did so!   36

Now to tell you the *plot*, which is the reason for my visit. First of all, this is the city of Cyrene – for that was the setting Diphilus chose. In that cottage over there, on an estate near the sea, lives Daemones, an old man of respectable character who came here in exile from Athens. It was not for any offence that he left his homeland; no, he got himself in something of a tangle while helping others, and through his own good nature he lost all his hard-earned savings. He also had a dear little daughter whom he lost. A wicked man bought her from a pirate, a dealer in women he was, and he brought her over here to Cyrene. Now a certain young Athenian, a fellow-citizen of Daemones here, saw her

one day going home from her music school, and fell
in love with her. He went off to the pimp who
owned her, and arranged to buy the girl for thirty
minas;[2] he duly paid a deposit and got the pimp to
seal the bargain with an oath.   55

Well, the pimp, true to character, didn't give two
hoots for this contract, or the oath he'd sworn to the
youth. He had a friend visiting him, a man as
crooked as himself, an old Sicilian rogue from Agri-
gentum, a really treacherous fellow. This man
started to sing the praises of the Athenian girl, and
indeed of all the other girls he owned. He began to
persuade him to accompany him back to Sicily –
said that the men there really enjoyed their pleas-
ures, and that he could make a pile of money, that
fortunes could be made from hiring out girls. Well,
he convinced him. They hired a boat on the sly,
and the pimp put all his goods on board under
cover of darkness. He told the young man who'd
bought the girl from him that he wanted to pay a
vow at the shrine of Venus – (*points*) this is it here –
and invited him there to lunch. In fact he went
straight off and boarded ship, and took away his
string of fillies with him! The young man heard
what had really happened – that the pimp had
done a bunk – so he went down to the harbour only
to find that the ship was miles out to sea.   77

When I saw the young girl being carried off, I
decided to come to her rescue – to save her, and
sink the pimp at the same time! I raised an
almighty gale and stirred up the waves of the deep.
For Arcturus is my name – and Arcturus is the
most violent of all constellations. I'm fierce when I
rise, and even fiercer when I set!

Now the pair of them, the pimp and his accom-
plice, are sitting on a rock like a couple of casta-
ways; their ship has been smashed to smithereens!
But the girl, and a companion of hers, another slavegirl, jumped from the ship in terror and got into
the lifeboat, and now the waves are carrying them

away from the reef and towards the shore where the old man's cottage stands, the old Athenian exile. In fact, the gale has blown all the slates off his roof!
Sceparnio comes out of the cottage carrying a spade.
The man who is coming out of the door now is his slave, Sceparnio, and the young man whom you will soon see coming this way is the one who bought the girl from the pimp.

    May you fare well – and may your enemies despair!   99

Arcturus goes off. Sceparnio moves about looking at the effects of last night's storm.

Sceparnio   Ye Gods above! What a gale Neptune sent us last night! The wind stripped the roof bare! Did I say 'wind'? – it wasn't a *wind*, so much; the way it stripped the roof of its tiles it was more like the typhoon in Euripides' *Alcmena*! Well, I suppose it's added a few windows and brightened up the inside a bit!
Sceparnio looks for a suitable place to dig. Plesidippus comes on with three friends in military dress.

Plesidip   All that for nothing! I've taken you away from your business and I wasn't able to catch that pimp at the harbour after all. It was all a wild goose chase! But I didn't want to give up without a struggle, you understand – that's why I've kept you all this time. Now I'm going to take a look at this shrine of Venus here, where he said he was going to make an offering.

Sceparnio   (*not seeing Plesidippus*) I suppose I'd better get this damned clay ready.

Plesidip   Hullo! Who's that?

Daemones comes out of his cottage.

Daemones   Hey, Sceparnio!
Sceparnio   Who's calling me?   119
Daemones   I am – the one who bought you – remember?
Sceparnio   Yes, yes, I'm your slave all right – don't remind me.

16

Daemones	(*ignoring the remark*) You need lots of clay, so dig really deep. I can see the whole roof needs recovering – it's got more holes in it than a sieve at the moment!
Plesidip	Good morning to you, father – to both of you, in fact.
Daemones	And to you.
Sceparnio	Why do you call him 'father' like that? You his son or his daughter?
Plesidip	Since I'm a man, I'm hardly likely to be his daughter, am I?
Sceparnio	Well, he's not your father, either! You'll have to look elsewhere!
Daemones	I did have a little daughter once, but I lost her, all I had. I never had any sons.
Plesidip	Well, perhaps the gods will give you one. 138
Sceparnio	I hope they give *you* something, too – a thick ear – whoever you are – taking up our time with your chit-chat when we've so much work to do!
Plesidip	(*to Daemones*) Do you live over there?
Sceparnio	What's it to you, eh? You looking the place over to come back later and strip it?
Plesidip	It must be a very valuable and superior sort of slave who can talk so rudely to a gentleman in his master's presence!
Sceparnio	And it's a boorish and boring man who can come to someone else's home, where he's got no business at all, and make such a nuisance of himself!
Daemones	Keep quiet, Sceparnio. What do you want, young man?
Plesidip	For a start, I'd give *him* a good hiding – so determined to have his say – in front of his own master, too! But – if it's not too much trouble – there are a few things I'd like to ask you.
Daemones	Well, there's work to do, but I'm listening.
Sceparnio	Why don't you go down to the swamp and cut some reeds for our roof while it's still fine? 159
Daemones	Quiet, you! (*To Plesidippus*) Now, tell me what it is you want, young man.
Plesidip	Tell me, have you seen a curly-headed man, with

17

	grey hair, a real rogue of a fellow, a lying, smooth-talking –
Daemones	(*looking at audience*) Plenty, plenty. It's because of fellows like him that I live the wretched life I do.
Plesidip	No, *here*, I mean, bringing two young ladies to the shrine of Venus. He was going to make an offering here – today ... or yesterday?
Daemones	No, young man. I haven't seen anyone sacrificing here for some time – and no one can sacrifice without my knowing; they're for ever wanting water, or something to light their fires, or cooking pans, or a knife or spit or a dish for the victim's entrails, or ... well, you know, there's always *something*! You'd think I'd bought my pots and dug my well for Venus, not for my own use! But no – there's been nothing for some days now.
Plesidip	If what you say is true, I've had it!
Daemones	Good heavens, there's nothing for you to fear here, I promise! 181
Sceparnio	Hey, you – hanging about the shrine here for a free meal? You'd better go tell your *own* slaves to get your dinner ready!
Daemones	Ah, were you perhaps invited to eat here, and your host didn't turn up?
Plesidip	*Precisely.*
Sceparnio	Well, push off home now – we don't care if you go hungry. It's Ceres you ought to be courting, not Venus! Venus is in charge of love – you can't make a meal of that!
Plesidip	(*exasperated*) This fellow is really insufferable!
Daemones	(*looks suddenly out to sea*) Ye Gods, Sceparnio, what's that? Those men by the shore there! *(Points)*
Sceparnio	Looks like some sort of farewell party to me.
Daemones	What? Why?
Sceparnio	Well, they all look pretty well soaked!
Daemones	They've been shipwrecked!
Sceparnio	Ah yes – and we've been wrecked, too, on dry land, roof, tiles and all! 200
Daemones	Look, look at them swimming for it! How frail they seem against that sea!

18

Plesidip Where – where are they?

Daemones Over there. (*Points to his right*) D'you see? By the shore.

Plesidip Oh, yes. (*To his friends*) Come on, follow me, men! I just hope that's the man I'm looking for, the filthy swine! (*To Daemones and Sceparnio*) Take care now!

Plesidippus and his friends go off.

Sceparnio No need to remind us: we will. (*Looks to another part of the coast*) But, good Lord, what's this I see?

Daemones What is it?

Sceparnio Two young women sitting all alone in a little boat! And they're in a terrible way, poor things! Good, good! *That* was lucky – a wave carried their boat away from the rocks towards the shore – a ship with a helmsman couldn't have done it better! I don't think I ever saw a bigger sea than this ... if they can make it through those breakers they'll be safe ... now, now ....this is the dangerous bit ... one's overboard! But wait, it's shallow there, she'll easily make it ... well done, *that*'s the way! She's up again, she's heading this way. It's all right! The other one has jumped out of the boat on to the shore. Look! See how shaky her knees were – she's fallen into the water again! But she's all right; now she's on dry land, too ... she's turned the other way, though ... damnation, *that*'s not the way! Oh, no! She'll get lost, that one, for sure. 228

Daemones (*losing interest*) What's it to you if she does?

Sceparnio (*still watching intently*) If she falls down the cliff she's heading for, she won't be wandering about for long!

Daemones If you reckon they'll give you your dinner, Sceparnio, you can stay and look after them. If you're intending to eat at my place, how about paying some attention to me?

Sceparnio (*tearing himself reluctantly away*) Fair enough, sir, fair enough.

Daemones This way, then. Come on.

Sceparnio All right, I'm coming.

19

*Daemones and Sceparnio go into the cottage. Palaestra
enters from stage left, dripping wet and close to exhaustion.
Her clothes are in shreds.*

Palaestra   When you hear tales of other people's misery,
You think them bad enough, but they're nothing
Compared with what you suffer in reality!   242
What have I done so awful that the gods
Have cast me out, in such a frightful state,
A stranger on an unknown shore? Is this
What I was born for, born to misery? Poor me!
Is this a fair reward for having tried
To live a decent life? If I had sinned
Against my parents or the gods, then I would think
All this was fair enough – but no, the truth is quite
The opposite. I have been careful never to offend;
So this is unfair treatment, cruel, unreasonable,
You gods are meting out! If this is how
You treat the innocent, what need the guilty fear?
For if I knew I or my parents had done wrong
To you, I should not think myself so wronged.
But now I am afflicted by my *master*'s crimes –
He is the cause of all my misery.
His ship is on the bottom of the sea, and all
He owned. I am the only thing he had   260
That's left; even the girl who shared the boat with
   me
Is lost, and I am all alone. If only she were safe
My plight would be less wretched – she could
   comfort me.
Now what have I left to hope for? I've no help,
No idea where to go ... in such a lonely spot!
Just roaring sea and rocks – no one will find me
   here!
These clothes are all I have, no food or hope
Of shelter. What is there left to live for now?
This place is quite unknown to me. If only someone
   came
And showed me how to find the way! Which way

To go – this way, or that? Oh dear! There's not a
    field
In sight, no sign of farming hereabouts.
Oh, I shall faint, I'm cold, I'm frightened and I'm
    lost!
My poor, poor parents, if you only knew
How wretched your poor daughter was! Freeborn I
    was,
Free as the day, and all for *this*! I might as well
Have been a slave for all the use my freedom was,
For all the joy my parents had of me!   278

*Palaestra all but faints with her grief. Ampelisca enters
from the other side, in a similar state.*

Ampelisca   No – there's nothing for it – best to end it all here
and now. I might as well. I can't go on like this –
I'm half dead with fright! The way things are, I've
lost every last hope I had. I've run around in every
direction, I've crawled into every possible hidey-
hole looking for my friend, I've been shouting and
listening and looking *everywhere*, trying to track her
down. But I can't find her anywhere, and I've no
idea where I'm going, or where else to look. I
haven't met a soul to ask, and this place, this whole
area, is about as deserted as deserted can be. But if
she's still alive, and there's still breath in me, I
mustn't rest until I find her.

Palaestra   (*alarmed*) I heard a voice nearby! Who's that?

Ampelisca   Oh Lord! Who's that I heard?

Palaestra   Lord help me, hope at last!

Ampelisca   Oh, if only this means some comfort!

Palaestra   I heard a woman's voice, surely?

Ampelisca   It's a woman! I heard a woman's voice!

Palaestra   Not – *Ampelisca*?

Ampelisca   Is it you – *Palaestra*?

Palaestra   I'll call her name. Ampelisca!   300

Ampelisca   Who *is* it?

Palaestra   Me! Palaestra!

Ampelisca   Where *are* you?

Palaestra   In ... desperate trouble, really I am!

21

Ampelisca	No more than I am – we're in this together, then. But I'm still trying to find where you are.
Palaestra	And I'm trying to find *you*.
Ampelisca	Let's follow our ears, then. (*Sings out*) Where *are* you?
Palaestra	Over here! Come on, this way!
Ampelisca	I'm doing my best.
Palaestra	Give me your hand.
Ampelisca	There!
Palaestra	Are you really alive, Ampelisca dear?
Ampelisca	Oh, now I can touch you again, you've given me something to live for! Oh, I can hardly *believe* I'm holding you in my arms again! Hold me tight, Palaestra dear! How much *brighter* you make everything seem!
Palaestra	You took the words right out of my mouth! But now we must get out of this place. 321
Ampelisca	But where to?
Palaestra	Let's follow the coastline.
Ampelisca	Wherever you like. But should we walk about in these sopping clothes?
Palaestra	We'll have to grin and bear it. *They move off. Palaestra suddenly halts in her tracks.* What on earth's this?
Ampelisca	What? Where?
Palaestra	On your right over there.
Ampelisca	It looks like some sort of shrine.
Palaestra	There must be people living nearby; it's such a pretty spot. God of this place – whoever you are – please, please help us out of our troubles; please come to the rescue of two poor, helpless, wretched women! *Ptolemocratia, priestess of Venus, comes out of the temple.*
Ptolemoc	Who is it who begs my Mistress's help? Surely I heard the voice of suppliants outside here? If so, the Goddess they call upon is good and kind, generous and gracious to all in trouble.
Palaestra	Good day to you, Holy Mother! 340
Ptolemoc	And to you, my girls! (*Looks at them*) But tell me, where have you been that your clothes are so wet,

	and you're in such a sorry state?
Palaestra	(*points*) We've come from over there, not far away. But before that – the place we started out from, is a long way off.
Ptolemoc	I presume, then, you have travelled on 'wooden steeds over the azure ways'?
Palaestra	Exactly.
Ptolemoc	It would have been better if you had come dressed in white, with offerings to make. Suppliants don't usually come to the shrine in such a sorry mess!
Palaestra	But we've been shipwrecked, both of us, cast ashore! Where do you think we could have found offerings to bring? (*They sink to the ground*) We're throwing ourselves at your mercy, take pity on us, please – we've nothing left, nothing to hope for, we don't even know where we are – we *implore* you, give us shelter and protect us and take pity on us! We've nowhere to go and we're absolutely desperate! We've got nothing in the world but what you can see!

362

Ptolemoc	Give me your hands. Get up, both of you. You'll find no woman has more compassion than I. But I've not much to offer you, I'm afraid; I live on little enough here. Mine is a frugal existence, girls; I serve Venus at my own expense.
Ampelisca	Is this *Venus*'s temple, then?
Ptolemoc	It is, and I am known as the custodian of the temple. I'll do whatever I can to make you welcome, so far as my slender resources allow. Come this way. (*She moves into the temple*)
Palaestra	It is good of you to welcome us in such a kindly way, mother.
Ptolemoc	No, it is no more than my duty.

They go inside. A group of Fishermen enters

Fishermen	The poor man lives a wretched life
	    There's little doubt about it;
	If 'e's learnt a trade 'e's got it made,
	    But 'e can't live well without it.

23

It's no good dreamin' of 'avin' a lot –   380
   'e 'as to make do with the little 'e's got!
Just look at us poor blighters 'ere –
   You can tell 'ow much *we* make a year!

These rods and 'ooks are the tools of our trade,
   In these we trust to earn a crust;
Each day we comes down to the sea from the town,
   And scratch about fer a decent catch.

No fancy wrestlin' schools fer us –
   The only exercise we gets
Is grapplin' with these fishin' nets –
   None of that smart gymnastic fuss!

Cockles and mussels and whelks and jellyfish,
   Seasnails, limpets, scaleyfish, shellyfish –
Our occupation's catchin' crustaceans
   Off the ocean floor, or the rocks of the shore!

But if our luck's out and there's no fish about,
   If when we've landed we're empty 'anded,
We slink back 'ome all wet and smelly
   And go to bed on an empty belly!

Just look at the way the sea's runnin' today!   400
   No chance fer us, it's plain.
We'll 'ave to make do with a winkle or two,
   Or go to bed without supper again!

Now, let's pay our respects to the Lady Venus 'ere, and ask 'er to bring us some luck today. (*They move towards the temple*)

Trachalio, slave of Plesidippus, comes along from the town – stage right.

Trachalio   I wonder where he is. I've looked for my master *everywhere* – I made sure not to miss him. When he left home he said he was off to the harbour and told me to meet him here at the temple of Venus ... Hullo, that's lucky, here are some people I can ask! Here goes, then. (*Adopting a mock-tragic style*) Good day to you, Sea Poachers, Captains of the Winkle

24

and Bent Pin Brigade – and what a famished crew
you look! How are things with you? As ... desperate as they seem?

Fishermen How do you *think* things are for fishermen? No food,
no drink, just disappointment.

Trachalio Tell me, have you seen a young man come this way
while you've been about – a determined looking
fellow, ruddy-faced, powerfully built? He had three
others with him – chaps in military cloaks, swords
and all.   422

Fishermen We haven't seen anyone round here like that, no.

Trachalio Or perhaps a bald old fellow, a proper Silenus,
fleshy, with a pot belly, shaggy eyebrows, and sort
of permanent frown? – a real crook this one, uni-
versally loathed, with a list of vices and villainy as
long as your arm. He had two pretty young ladies
with him.

Fishermen A man with qualifications like that shouldn't be
going to a temple of Venus – the *gallows* would be
more like it!

Trachalio But have you seen him? Tell me.

Fishermen No one's been here at all. Goodbye!

The Fishermen go off.

Trachalio Goodbye ... *Just* as I thought. *Just* as I expected!
The master's been taken for a ride, and that pimp
has done a flit, the blighter! He's sailed off and
taken the girls with him. I must be clairvoyant!
And he actually invited the master to a meal here,
the devious, deceitful *devil*!... Now all I can do is
wait here for master to arrive. If I see the priestess
of Venus I could ask her if she knows anything.
She's bound to tell me.   443

Ampelisca comes out of the temple with an empty pitcher.

Ampelisca (*to priestess inside*) I see, yes. I'm to knock at the
cottage next door here and ask for some water.

Trachalio Hullo! Whose voice is that?

Ampelisca (*startled*) Oh! Who's that?

Trachalio (*seeing a pretty girl*) And who's *that*? Is it – *Ampelisca*
coming out of the temple?

Ampelisca	Is it – *Trachalio*, Plesidippus's man?
Trachalio	It *is*!
Ampelisca	It *is*! Trachalio, hullo!
Trachalio	Ampelisca! Hullo! What are you doing here?
Ampelisca	Not enjoying life as a young girl should, *I* can tell you.
Trachalio	Don't talk like that – it's unlucky!
Ampelisca	We're adults, aren't we? I'm only telling the truth. But what about you and your master Plesidippus – where is he?
Trachalio	Eh? Oh, come on, he's inside, isn't he? In *there*. (*Points to temple*)
Ampelisca	No he most definitely *isn't*. Not a sign of him! 461
Trachalio	He didn't come?
Ampelisca	That's the truth.
Trachalio	Hm, not something I know much about!... How long before dinner's ready?
Ampelisca	*What* dinner?
Trachalio	Well, you're sacrificing here, aren't you?
Ampelisca	Eh? What are you talking about?
Trachalio	Look: Labrax, your master, invited my master Plesidippus here for dinner. That's a fact.
Ampelisca	I'm not surprised. He swindles everybody, that one – even the gods themselves! It's all in a day's work for a pimp!
Trachalio	Aren't you offering a sacrifice here, then, you and your master?
Ampelisca	(*impatiently*) How did you guess?
Trachalio	What *are* you doing here, then?
Ampelisca	We were in terrible trouble and danger, and fearing for our lives ... we were absolutely helpless and had no one to turn to ... and then the priestess of Venus here saved us and took us in ... me and Palaestra. 482
Trachalio	*Palaestra?* Is she here – my master's girl?
Ampelisca	That's right.
Trachalio	My dear girl, that really is *marvellous* news! But tell me about it – that danger you were in. I'd like to hear.
Ampelisca	Last night, Trachalio, our ship was wrecked!

Trachalio	A ship? A *ship*? What are you talking about?
Ampelisca	Haven't you heard how the pimp tried to take us off to Sicily? He put every last thing he had on board ship – and now it's gone, the whole lot!
Trachalio	Bless you, Neptune! That was neat work! There's no better thrower of dice than you in existence – one perfect throw and you put paid to the perisher! Where is he now, the pimp?
Ampelisca	Died of drink, I reckon. Neptune was serving it up in bucketsful last night!
Trachalio	Yes, no choice either! Lord! Oh, Ampelisca, *bless* you! What sweet news this makes – words like honey-wine – sweet as you are, my love! But tell me, how did you and Palaestra reach safety? 502
Ampelisca	I'll tell you. When we saw we were being driven on to the rocks, we were both terrified; we jumped down out of the ship into the lifeboat. I quickly untied the rope in the general panic, and the storm carried us off, away from the rest. So all night long we were tossed about by the wind and waves – we had a terrible time, *terrible*! Well, finally we were blown ashore this morning, only half alive!
Trachalio	Ah, yes, that's Neptune all over; he's like a finicky customs officer: any doubtful goods, and he sees they go straight over the side!
Ampelisca	Oh, go and take a running jump at yourself!
Trachalio	You too, dear!... I just *knew* the pimp would do this – and he has. I *said* he would, more than once. There's nothing for it, I'll grow my hair long and set up as a fortune-teller!
Ampelisca	If you knew so much, why didn't you and your master do something to stop him getting away?
Trachalio	What *could* he have done? 521
Ampelisca	What could he have done? You really want to know? If he *really* loved Palaestra he should have kept watch night and day, he should have been on guard all the time. Not Plesidippus, though! You can judge how much he thinks of her from the way he's behaved!
Trachalio	Why do you say that?

27

Ampelisca	It's obvious.
Trachalio	Look: imagine a fellow going to the baths. Even if he keeps a sharp eye on his clothes, he has them stolen all the same. He doesn't know which of the crowd to watch. It's easy for the thief: *he* knows who's looking out for him. But the fellow keeping an eye on his clothes doesn't know who *he* is! Don't you see? ... Now take me to Palaestra.
Ampelisca	Just go into the temple of Venus here – you'll find her sitting there, crying her heart out. 538
Trachalio	Dear me, I'm sorry to hear that. Why is she crying?
Ampelisca	She's terribly upset; the pimp took the little box of trinkets she had; she had some means of identifying her parents in it. She's worried it may be lost for ever.
Trachalio	Where was the box?
Ampelisca	In the ship along with us. The pimp locked it up in a trunk, so she shouldn't ever be able to find her parents.
Trachalio	That's a filthy trick – forcing a freeborn girl to live like a slave!
Ampelisca	Now it's obviously gone down to the bottom with the ship. All the pimp's gold and silver's in the same place, too.
Trachalio	Well, I dare say someone's dived down and fished it out.
Ampelisca	That's why she's so wretched, because she's lost her trinkets, poor thing!
Trachalio	All the more reason for me to go in and cheer her up; she really mustn't take it so hard. 'Keep hoping', that's what I say. You never know what's round the corner! 560
Ampelisca	And I say: 'Hope for too much and it's disappointment round the corner!'
Trachalio	All right, then. Try this one: 'The best tonic for trouble is to stay cool.' Now, if you'll excuse me, I'll go in.

Trachalio goes into the temple.

Ampelisca	You go ... Now I'll do what the priestess said, and

28

ask for water next door here. She said they'd give
me some straight away if I said it was for her. I
don't think I've ever met a nicer old girl – one who
deserves more than she does all the blessings
heaven and earth can give. How *sweet* she was! How
kind and gracious to us! We were frightened,
sopping wet, and half dead when she took us in –
but it didn't bother her a bit. She treated us as if we
were her own daughters! Fancy her tucking up her
clothes like that as she heated up some water for us
to wash! But I mustn't keep her waiting. I'd better
get the water. (*She knocks on the door*) Hullo? Anyone
at home? Open up! Anyone in?

The slave Sceparnio comes out.

Sceparnio	Who's that thumping on our door?	580
Ampelisca	Me.	
Sceparnio	Hullo! Here's a piece of luck! A woman – and a very pretty one, too!	
Ampelisca	Good morning, young man.	
Sceparnio	And a very good morning to you, young lady!	
Ampelisca	I've come –	
Sceparnio	And you're welcome. But ... come back later on, this evening, dear. Then I can really look after you properly. I can't manage much so early in the day. Well, what do you say, my pretty little love? (*He caresses her*)	
Ampelisca	Hey! Not so free with your hands!	
Sceparnio	Gods above, she's the very *image* of Venus! Look at that sparkle in her eyes – Lord! – and what a figure! Such lovely colouring, too – a real dusty – no, *dusky* beauty – that's right! And those *breasts*! Those luscious *lips*! (*He grabs her*)	
Ampelisca	Keep your hands off! I'm not the town trollop, you know!	
Sceparnio	Can't I just give you ... a nice little squeeze, like that? You're such a *cuddly* little thing!	600
Ampelisca	Yes, yes; when I've got time, we'll have some fun and games. But now I've come on an errand; so, tell me, are you going to help me or not?	

Sceparnio	What do you want?
Ampelisca	If you had any sense you could *see* what I want! (*Points to pitcher*)
Sceparnio	If *you* had any sense – he, he! – you could see what *I* want!
Ampelisca	The priestess of Venus told me to ask for some water here.
Sceparnio	Well, *I'm* the big noise round here, and you won't get a drop unless you *beg* me for it. We dug that well of ours at our own expense, with our own tools. You won't get a drop of water from me unless you *grovel*!
Ampelisca	Why are you so mean? I only want a jug of water. People give even their *enemies* that!
Sceparnio	Why are *you* so mean? What I want is normal between *any* two consenting adults!
Ampelisca	Look, I'm not being mean, love. I'll do whatever you want. <div align="right">620</div>
Sceparnio	(*aside*) He, he! I'm home and dry; she's already calling me her love! (*Aloud*) You'll get your water: fair's fair. Let's have the jug.
Ampelisca	There. Hurry up and bring it back, please.
Sceparnio	Wait here: I'll be right back, darling.

Sceparnio goes in.

Ampelisca	What excuse can I give the priestess for taking so long? (*She looks towards the sea*) Oh! How terrified I am even when I look at that sea! (*Suddenly her tone changes*) Oh *no*! What's that I can see on the shore over there? It's my master, the pimp, and his Sicilian friend! Oh *dear*, and I thought they'd both been drowned! That means more trouble than we'd thought. I must run inside the temple and tell Palaestra; we'll have to take refuge at the altar before the old devil gets here and catches us. I'm off *now* – this is really serious! <div align="right">636</div>

Ampelisca runs into the temple. Sceparnio comes out again with the water.

Sceparnio	Ye Gods – I never thought any pleasure could come

from *water* before – but I really enjoyed pulling this up! The well didn't seem anything like as deep as it used to be. Up it came, no trouble at all ... but hark at me! I'm a sly one – fancy falling head over heels like this – right out of the blue! (*Not seeing Ampelisca is no longer there*) There's your water, my little beauty. There, now, carry it *properly*, like this (*puts it on his head and wiggles his bottom*)– that's how I like it done! Eh? Where are you? *You*'re a saucy one! Come on, come and get your water!... Where *are* you?... She's fallen for me, I really think she has! The little minx is hiding ... Where *are* you? Are you going to fetch this jug? Where *are* you?... Playing games with me, are you?... Now look here, *are* you going to fetch this jug? Where the blazes are you?... Damn me, I can't see her anywhere! She's making a fool of me ... I'll put the jug down here, right in the middle of the road. But wait – supposing someone pinches it! That's a sacred jug of Venus's! No – there'd be *hell* to pay. That priestess woman – I wonder if she's setting a trap to catch me with one of the sacred jugs! If anyone sees me with this ... they'll clap me in irons and *do* for me! They'd have every right to, too! (*Turns it over*) Wait a moment – there's an inscription on it. Yes – it says who its owner is, plain enough. I'm going to call the priestess out of the temple and get her to take this jug back! (*He goes up to the doors of the temple*) Hey! Hullo! Ptolemocratia! Come on out here and get your jug! Some young woman brought it over to me. (*No reply*) It's no good – I'll have to take it in. This is great fun, I *must* say: I pick all the best jobs. I pull the water from the well, now I've got to heave it about for them, too!   671

Sceparnio goes into the temple. The pimp Labrax enters, followed by his friend Charmides. Both are dripping wet and utterly miserable.

Labrax If you want to end up out of luck and out of pocket, just throw in your lot with Neptune! Have any dealings with him, and this is the way he sends you back home! Well, no wonder: they say Liberty and Hercules never were travelling companions.[3] Where's that partner of mine? This mess was all his fault. Ah, here he is!

Charmides Where the devil are you rushing to, Labrax? I can't keep up if you go so fast. 680

Labrax Damn you, I wish you'd come unstuck in Sicily before ever I set eyes on you! It's all your fault I'm in such a mess!

Charmides And I wish I'd been dragged off to jail instead of being invited to your house that day! For the rest of your life I hope the gods send you guests just like yourself!

Labrax When I took you in, I opened the door to an agent of doom all right! Why on earth was I such a damned fool as to listen to you? Why did I ever leave home, or get on board that ship? I've lost all I ever owned in it – no, more, *more*!

Charmides No wonder the ship got wrecked, I say! Carrying filthy scum like you, and all your filthy, ill-gotten gains!

Labrax It was listening to all your smooth talk that proved my undoing!

Charmides That dinner you gave me was the filthiest I ever had – filthier than the ones Thyestes and Tereus ate![4] 700

Labrax Oh God! I feel sick! Please – hold my head!

Charmides Let it all go! Heave your lungs up, for all I care!

Labrax Ugh! (*Brightening a little*) ... I wonder where Palaestra and Ampelisca are now.

Charmides Feeding the fishes on the bottom of the briny, I should think!

Labrax You've reduced me to beggary – it's all *your* doing. Why did I ever listen to your big talk, your loud-mouthed lying?

Charmides You should be grateful to me: you were a witless wet before – but, now you're even *wetter*, you seem *wittier*, too! All my own work!

Labrax	Why don't you – go to blazes and leave me alone?
Charmides	Why don't *you*? I was just going to make the same suggestion myself.
Labrax	Oh God! What a mess to be in! Who could be worse off than me?
Charmides	*I* could – I'm much worse off than you, Labrax.
Labrax	Why?
Charmides	Because I don't deserve all this: you *do*! 720
Labrax	I never thought I'd want to swap places with a bulrush, but it seems a good idea now. At least they stay high and dry!
Charmides	(*teeth chattering*) I feel as if I'm in training for the army! I'm sh-shivering s-so much everything I say ... s-s-sounds like a d-d-division d-doing drill!
Labrax	Lord, Neptune, that was a cold bath you gave us! Ever since I left you I've been freezing – even with all these clothes on!
Charmides	He doesn't even serve hot drinks, either. His drinks are only one sort: salt water on the rocks!
Labrax	Think how lucky blacksmiths are: they're always warm round their fireplaces!
Charmides	Think how nice it'd be to be a duck: they're bone-dry as soon as they get out of the water!
Labrax	I suppose I could always hire myself out as the Human Alligator at a fair!
Charmides	Human Alligator?
Labrax	Yes: just look at the way I'm gnashing my teeth!
Charmides	I suppose I thoroughly deserved to be cleaned up like this. 741
Labrax	Why?
Charmides	For ever having agreed to go on board ship with the likes of you! Why – you roused the whole sea to fury against me!
Labrax	The whole thing was *your* idea! You promised me we'd make a packet in Sicily hiring out my girls; you said we'd be making it hand over fist!
Charmides	You filthy swine, did you expect to swallow up the whole of Sicily just like that?
Labrax	Swallow up? Some whale or other's done the swallowing up – and he's had my trunk, stuffed with all

33

	that gold and silver!
Charmides	I expect it's the same one that had the wallet full of silver I was carrying in my bag.
Labrax	This really is the *end*! All I have left in the world is this one little tunic and this pathetic cloak! I'm absolutely ruined!
Charmides	Well, we can team up together if you like. We're a good match!

760

Labrax	If only my girls were safe there'd be some hope left. But as it is, if young Plesidippus finds me, he's going to make trouble, and soon! I took a down-payment for Palaestra from him!
Charmides	What are you moaning for, you booby? Lord, as long as you've a tongue in your head, you can talk your way out of *anything*!

Sceparnio comes out of the temple.

Sceparnio	What on earth's going on here, that's what I'd like to know – two girls in Venus's temple here clinging to her statue for dear life and crying their eyes out! I wonder what the poor things are so scared of. They tell me they were shipwrecked last night and cast ashore this morning.
Labrax	(*overhearing*) Wha – *what*'s that you say, young fellow? Where are these girls you're talking about?
Sceparnio	In Venus's temple here.
Labrax	How many of them?
Sceparnio	Oh, no more than you and me!
Labrax	Then they must be mine!
Sceparnio	*Must* be? I don't know about that.

780

Labrax	What do they look like?
Sceparnio	Not bad! I wouldn't say no to either of them . . . if I was drunk enough!
Labrax	You're sure they're *young* girls?
Sceparnio	I'm sure you're a damn nuisance! Go and see for yourself if you want!
Labrax	Charmides, old boy, they've *got* to be my girls in there!
Charmides	To hell with you! I don't care whether they are or whether they aren't!

Labrax   I'm going to break into the temple now – I'll *rush* 'em!

Charmides   Oh, rush into a bottomless pit – do me a favour! (*To Sceparnio*) I say, could you find me a place somewhere to sleep, my dear chap?

Sceparnio   Sleep right where you are, wherever you like! No one's stopping you – it's public property.

Charmides   But look at me – you can see my clothes are soaking! Take me home with you and give me some dry clothes while my own are drying – I'll pay you back some day.   801

Sceparnio   There's this bit of blanket – it's the only thing I've got that's dry. I'll give you that if you like – I use it as a cloak, or as an overcoat if it rains. You give me your clothes, and I'll get them dried.

Charmides   Oh, no you don't! I've been cleaned out once already at sea – are you trying to take me to the cleaners again – on dry land?

Sceparnio   Cleaned out, *wiped* out, I really couldn't care less! I'm not giving you a thing unless I get something in return. You can sweat to death or freeze to death, be sick as well – it's all the same to me. I'm not having a stranger as guest in my house, and that's flat.   814

Sceparnio goes into the house.

Charmides   Hey, *wait!* . . . He must've been in the slave trade, that one, whoever he is – not one shred of pity in the whole of his body! But what's the point of my standing here all miserable and wet? Why don't I go into the temple here and sleep off that skinful I drank last night – it was far too much, I knew it at the time. Neptune was pouring sea-water down our throats as if he was blending Greek wines! It was his way of cleaning us right out, I suppose – by giving us a dose of his salts. I can tell you, if he'd kept us drinking a little longer, we'd have passed out there and then! As it was, he packed us off home – more dead than alive! . . . Now I'll go and see what my drinking-mate, the pimp, is up to inside.

Charmides goes into the temple. Daemones comes out of his cottage.

Daemones What strange games the gods do play with us mortals! Such strange dreams they send us! They won't even let us *sleep* in peace! Take *me*, for instance: last night I had a really mystifying dream. I dreamed I saw an ape trying to climb up to a swallow's nest; but it couldn't reach to pull the chicks out; so then it came up to me, this ape, and asked me to lend it a ladder! I said no. I told it all swallows were the children of Philomela and Procne,[5] and begged her not to harm my fellow-countrymen. Then it became really angry, and seemed to be threatening to do me a mischief. It actually summoned me to court! Well, then I got angry, too; I grabbed the ape around the middle, and put the disgusting beast in chains! ... What the meaning of all *that* might be I still haven't a clue – it's been puzzling me all day!   846
There is a noise off in the temple.
But what's all that din in the temple next door? I've never heard anything like it!

Trachalio runs wildly out of the temple.

Trachalio (*mock tragic*) Help! Citizens of Cyrene, save us, I beg you! Yokels, locals – everyone who lives hereabouts – defend the defenceless, smash to smithereens a soulless sinner! To the rescue! Stop the power of the perverted prevailing over these poor impotent innocents! Give impurity its proper punishment, and decency the reward it deserves! See that men here live by the law, not as victims bullied by brute force! Hurry to the temple of Venus – help, I beg you all once more, all that are nearby and hear my cry! Come to the aid of those who by ancient custom have entrusted themselves to the safekeeping of Venus and her priestess! Wring the neck of unrighteousness before it reaches you and wrings yours! 863

Daemones What's all that about?

Trachalio Sir, I beg you by your knees, whoever you are –

Daemones Just leave my knees out of this and tell me why you're making all this noise!

Trachalio I beg you, I *beseech* you, if you hope to get a bumper crop of silphium and silphium juice[6] this year, and to export it to Capua safe and sound, and to be free for ever from runny eyes –

Daemones Are you *mad*?

Trachalio – or if you expect a good harvest of silphium *seed*, that you won't begrudge me the favour I shall beg of you, sir!

Daemones And *I* beseech *you*, by your legs and ankles and the skin of your back, if you *don't* want a whacking bundle of elm rods, and a really huge crop of beatings this year – *tell* me why you're making such a din! 881

Trachalio (*taken aback*) Why are you being so nasty? I wished you all sorts of *good* things!

Daemones I'm the very opposite of nasty: I'm praying you get what you deserve!

Trachalio Well, listen to this, then – I'm *begging* you!

Daemones What's the matter?

Trachalio There are two innocent women inside there, and they need your help. They've been shamefully wronged – they *are* being wronged, and it's illegal and unfair – and all this is going on inside the temple of Venus! And the priestess of Venus is being insulted as well!

Daemones What? Who could be so rash as to dare lay hands on the priestess? Who are these women? How are they being wronged?

Trachalio You listen and I'll tell you. They're clinging to the statue of Venus. But now this unscrupulous fellow is trying to tear them away from it. And by rights both of them should be free! 900

Daemones	*What?* Is there a man alive with so little regard for the gods?
Trachalio	Yes. He's a liar, a criminal, a monster, a habitual perjurer, a filthy, lawless, shameless, godless – well, in a word, he's a *pimp*! Could I say worse?
Daemones	My God, from what you say he *really* has it coming to him!
Trachalio	Yes – the sort of man who could try to throttle a priestess!
Daemones	Heavens, he shan't get away with it, though! Turbalio! Sparax! Come on out here! Where are you?
Trachalio	Go on in, please! Go and help them!
Daemones	(*still shouting*) I shan't tell you twice! *Two big slaves come on.* Follow me, this way.
Trachalio	Go on – tell them to bash his eyes out – just like cooks do to cuttle-fish!
Daemones	Toss him out here by the heels like a stuck pig!

Daemones goes into the temple with the slaves.

Trachalio	Listen to that noise! The pimp's being pounded to pulp! Well, I hope they knock all the teeth out of his head, the rotten sod! Ah, here come the women out of the temple, poor frightened things! 921

Palaestra and Ampelisca rush out of the temple in despair.

Palaestra	Now we are utterly bereft Of everything, there's nothing left, No chance of rescue or of aid, No hope of safety. We're afraid We do not even know Which way to go! We are quite petrified At the outrageous way Our cruel master has Treated us all inside! Pulling the old priestess about Without the slightest inhibition – Manhandling her without A thought for her position! Then, dragging us by might and main

From the image of the goddess where
We both had clung – in vain!
And now, seeing that fate
Has brought us to our knees,   940
And made us desperate,
What better way to end
Our wretchedness than die?
When things are black as this
Death is the only remedy!

Trachalio What sort of talk is that? I must go and cheer them up. Hey, Palaestra!

Palaestra Who is that?

Trachalio Ampelisca!

Ampelisca Lord, who can it be?

Palaestra Who's that calling our names?

Trachalio Look round here and you'll see.

Palaestra Oh, hope at last! We may be saved yet!

Trachalio Sh! Cheer up, do! Leave everything to me!

Palaestra Ah, if only I *could* forget the threat of mischief – it's that that threatens to make me do *myself* a mischief!

Trachalio Now, now, stop it, you really are being silly!

Palaestra And you stop trying to talk me out of it! After all I've been through! If you haven't got some sort of trick up your sleeve, Trachalio, we're as good as finished!   961

Ampelisca I'd rather *die* than have that pimp let loose on me! But then I'm only a woman, after all – when I think of death I just tremble all over! Lord, what an *awful* day this has been!

Trachalio You must both be brave.

Palaestra *Brave*? Where on earth do I get the strength to be brave with?

Trachalio Look: don't be frightened. Just sit by the altar here.

Ampelisca How is this altar going to do us any more good than the statue of Venus inside the temple? We were clinging to it just a moment ago, and we were torn from it by force!

Trachalio Just sit here. I'll look after you. Think of this altar as your camp. (*Paces it out*) These are your ramparts, and I'll be on guard duty, protecting you.

	With Venus's help, I'll make a stand against the iniquitous forces of the pimp! 978
Palaestra	All right, we'll do as you say. And, kind Venus, we both beseech you, as we cling weeping to your altar, on our knees we beg you to take us under your care and keep us safe! And take vengeance, we pray, on the wicked one who has insulted your shrine, and, by your leave, allow us to take refuge at your altar here! Do not be insulted, or hold us to blame if you think we are less clean than we might be. Neptune supervised the bathing last night – so it's his fault if we're not as we should be!
Trachalio	That's a fair request, Venus, I think, and one you ought to grant. It's only right you should pardon them – they're only behaving like this because they're so frightened. According to the story, you were born of a shell-fish yourself – so don't turn your back on these two little ... *cockles*! ... Good! Here comes the old boy who's been so kind to us.

Daemones comes out of the temple, followed by two slaves with Labrax.

Daemones	Out of the temple, come on, you sacrilegious monster! You two girls can go and sit at the altar – where are they?
Trachalio	Over here, look! 999
Daemones	Good! That's where I wanted them. Just let him go near them now! (*To Labrax*) Think you can flout the laws of heaven and get away with it, do you – while we look on? (*To one of the slaves*) Give him one in the face!

Slave punches Labrax.

Labrax	You won't get away with this!
Daemones	Dares to threaten me, does he – the *nerve* of the fellow!
Labrax	This is outrageous! I've got my rights. You can't take away my girls. This is robbery!
Trachalio	You take any respectable senator of Cyrene here, and ask him if these girls ought to be yours or ought to be free – and if *you* oughtn't to be clapped in jail

and spend the rest of your natural life there – till
you've worn the floor out with your perpetual
pacing!

Labrax Well, I didn't reckon on bandying words with scum
like *him*! (*To Daemones*) It's you I'm talking to.

Daemones You argue the matter with him first – he's the one
who knows you.

Labrax *You*'re the one I'll deal with. 1020

Trachalio But you've got to deal with *me*, I'm afraid! These
are your girls, are they?

Labrax They are.

Trachalio Go on, then – just you touch one of them with ...
so much as the tip of your little finger –

Labrax Well, what if I do?

Trachalio I'll turn you into a punch-bag, damn me if I don't!
I'll string you up and pepper you with punches,
you filthy pervert!

Labrax (*to Daemones*) Are you saying I can't take my own
girls from that altar?

Daemones No, you can't. We have a law which says –

Labrax *Damn* your laws, they mean nothing to me! I'm
taking those girls with me – both of them, this
instant. As for you, old fellow – if you've taken a
fancy to them, it'll cost you a pile – in hard cash.
Or Venus can keep them, if she likes them so much
– but she'll have to pay up, too! 1038

Daemones Venus pay *you*? Now you listen carefully to me: if
you use the least bit of violence on them, even as a
joke, I'll pack you off home in such a pickle you
won't recognise yourself! (*To slaves*) You two –
when I give you the nod, poke his eyes out, or I'll
wrap the whips round you tighter than the lashing
round bundles of myrtle!

Labrax This is ... common assault!

Trachalio Oh, you object to assault, do you – a filthy felon
like *you*?

Labrax And you dare insult me, a dyed-in-the-wool crook
like *you*?

Trachalio All right, then, I don't mind – I'm a crook, and
you're a pillar of society! But does that mean these

41

	two girls shouldn't be free?	
Labrax	Free? What, *them*?	
Trachalio	Yes, free, I tell you! They're your betters! They're Greek citizens! This one here was born in Athens, of free Athenian parents.	
Labrax	What's that you say?	
Trachalio	This girl – she's a freeborn Athenian.	
Daemones	Lord! A compatriot of mine?	1060
Trachalio	Aren't you a Cyrenean?	
Daemones	No, an Athenian, born and bred in Athens.	
Trachalio	Well, for pity's sake, sir – protect your fellow-citizens!	
Daemones	(*emotionally*) O, my poor daughter! When I look at this young woman, she reminds me of you, and all the heartache you caused me! Only three years old, she was, when I lost her! She'd be about the same age as this girl, too, if she were still alive!	
Labrax	Look, I paid good money for the two of them – wherever they come from. What difference is it to me whether they were born in Athens or Thebes – or anywhere, so long as they serve me as servants should?	
Trachalio	So *that*'s what you think, is it, you filthy slave-trader you! Keep freeborn children stolen from their parents and put them to work in your vile trade, would you? I don't know where the other girl comes from, but one thing I do know: she's better class than *your* sort – you stinking scum!	1080
Labrax	(*ironically*) Oh, they belong to you, then, do they?	
Trachalio	All right, let's see who's telling the truth. If your back hasn't got more welts than a man o'war's got nails, I'm lying in my teeth. Then, when I've had a look at yours, you take a look at mine. If it's not as smooth as the smoothest, finest-quality hide a flask-maker could wish to use – well, you can … let me tan your hide to exhaustion! What are you gaping at the girls for? Forget them. Touch them once and I'll tear your eyes out!	
Labrax	Save your breath. I'm taking them both with me. (*Moves towards the cottage*)	

Daemones	What are you going to do?
Labrax	Get Vulcan to do his stuff – he's no friend of Venus's![7]
Trachalio	Where's he off to?
Labrax	(*shouting*) Hullo? Anyone in? *Hullo?*
Daemones	Touch that door and I'll cut you down! I'll pitch into you with my fists for forks!
Slave	There's no fire around here, anyway – dried figs is all we get to eat! 1100
Daemones	I'll give you a fire all right – if I can have your head as the hearth!
Labrax	Then I'll go and look for it elsewhere.
Daemones	And when you find it?
Labrax	I'm going to build a big fire here!
Daemones	To cauterise yourself, you monster?
Labrax	No – to burn these two girls alive at the altar, that's what!
Daemones	Damn me if I won't grab you by the beard, throw you on top of the fire and sling you out half-cooked for vultures to feed on! (*Aside*) And now I come to think of it, *this* must be the ape in my dream, and these are the two swallows he wants to pull out of their nest!
Trachalio	(*to Daemones*) Will you do something for me, sir? Watch over the girls, don't let any harm come to them, while I fetch my master here.
Daemones	Very well. Go and find your master and bring him here.
Trachalio	Be careful now. This fellow – 1120
Daemones	If he touches them, or even *looks* as if he might, he'll very much regret it!
Trachalio	Careful, then.
Daemones	Don't worry. Off with you!
Trachalio	Watch *him* – don't let him escape either. We stand to pay a fortune if we don't produce him in court today.
Daemones	I'll see to everything. Just you go.
Trachalio	I'll be right back.

Trachalio goes.

43

Daemones	It's your choice, pimp – are you going to keep quiet of your own free will, or do you want a thrashing?
Labrax	I don't give a damn for your threats, grandad, I'm taking my girls, whether you or Venus or Jove Almighty like it or not!
Daemones	Just you touch them.
Labrax	I will, too.
Daemones	Go on, then – take *one* step towards them!
Labrax	You tell those two heavies to step out of my way!
Daemones	No, no, they're stepping *your* way!
Labrax	They'd better not, I tell you! 1140
Daemones	And what are *you* going to do about it?
Labrax	Er – er – I'll step out of *their* way! (*Angrily*) But if I ever catch you in the city, you old fool, I'll never answer to the name 'pimp' again if I don't make a proper fool of you before I have done!
Daemones	Yes, yes, you do that. In the meantime, you touch those girls and you'll get a king-sized hiding!
Labrax	*What*-sized?
Daemones	Pimp-sized, *that*'s what!
Labrax	I don't give a damn for your threats. I'm taking both the girls with me whether you like it or not.
Daemones	Touch them, then.
Labrax	I will, too.
Daemones	You will, will you? – well, see what you get for it! Quick Turbalio – get a couple of clubs from the house.
Labrax	(*alarmed*) Clubs?
Daemones	Good thick ones! Quick as you can! *One of the slaves, Turbalio, goes into the house.* (*To Labrax*) I'll see you get the reception you deserve, by God! 1160
Labrax	Curses! I'd have liked to oblige you, but ... (*In stage military voice*) I seem to have left me fightin' tackle on board ship!... Can I just *speak* to the girls?
Daemones	No, you can't. *Turbalio enters with two clubs.* Ah good, here comes our club-swinger!
Labrax	Help! My head's singing already!

44

RUDENS

Daemones Go on, Sparax – grab that other club and one of you stand here, the other there, both of you, quick ... closer ... that's it. Now listen. If he lays so much as a finger on them, you lay into him so hard with those clubs of yours that he doesn't even know the way home – or else I'll do for the pair of you! If he tries to speak to either of them, you answer for them – but stay where you are. If he tries to get away, jump to it and wrap those cudgels of yours round his legs!

Labrax Won't they let me even run away?

Daemones I've made myself quite clear. (*To slaves*) Trachalio's gone to fetch his master – as soon as he gets back, you can go off home. That's all. See you do *exactly* as I've told you, now.   1182

Daemones goes into the cottage.

Labrax Hell's *teeth*! These temples change their allegiance pretty quickly! It was Venus's just a moment ago – now it's more like Hercules', to judge from these two club-swinging statues the old man's put up outside! Dammit, I don't know *where* I can go now – trouble at sea, now trouble on land! Trouble in *every* damn direction! (*Changing tactics*) Palaestra! Hullo?

Turbalio (*in a deep voice*) What do you want?

Labrax Eh? *That* can't be right. That's not my Palaestra speaking! (*Tries again*) Ampelisca!

Sparax Just watch it! (*Moves towards him threateningly*)

Labrax (*eyeing them nervously*) Not bad advice, either, from two useless clods like them! (*Aloud*) Hey, you two, I'm talking to you. Listen. No harm in going a little nearer the girls, is there?

Turbalio None – so far as *we*'re concerned.

Labrax Er – what about as far as *I*'m concerned?

Turbalio None at all – so long as you watch out.   1200

Labrax Watch out for what?

Turbalio (*swinging club*) *This!* A real pasting, *that*'s what!

Labrax Let me out of here, for pity's sake!

Turbalio Go, if you want.

Labrax That's decent of you, thanks ... much obliged ...

45

Turbalio and Sparax threaten him.
... but I'll stick around, I think! You stay where
you are.
Turbalio and Sparax stand back again.
My God, this really hasn't been my lucky day! But
my mind's made up: I'll have to starve 'em out!

*Trachalio re-enters with Plesidippus. They are conversing
excitedly.*

Plesidip	That pimp laid hands on my girl, did he? Tried to tear her from Venus's altar?
Trachalio	Exactly.
Plesidip	Why didn't you kill him on the spot?
Trachalio	I didn't have a sword handy.
Plesidip	You could have used a club, or a stone?
Trachalio	What? Chase scum like this with stones like a dog? Too good for him!
Labrax	Oh help! I've had it now – here's Plesidippus. He'll wipe the floor with me, he'll make *mincemeat* of me –
Plesidip	Were the girls sitting at the altar when you came to fetch me? 1221
Trachalio	Yes, they're still there.
Plesidip	Who's guarding them?
Trachalio	Some old gentleman who lives next door to the temple. He was really kind. He's guarding them now with his slaves – I told him what to do.
Plesidip	Take me straight to the pimp. Where is the fellow?
Labrax	Good day to you!
Plesidip	Damn your good days! Just take your pick and be smart about it. Do you want to be hauled away peaceably – or dragged off with a rope round your neck? Choose, while you've still got the chance.
Labrax	I don't like the sound of either!
Plesidip	Right, Trachalio – you run down to the shore and tell those men to come to the city and meet me at the harbour – the ones I brought with me to hand this fellow over to the hangman. Then come back here and keep watch. I'm going to take this filthy crook to court!

Trachalio goes.

	(*To Labrax*) Come on – you're coming to court with me! 1241
Labrax	What have I done wrong?
Plesidip	What – ? You took a deposit from me for the girl, then took her away with you!
Labrax	Er – I didn't actually take her *away*.
Plesidip	Eh? You *deny* it?
Labrax	Well, I took her *on board*, yes – but I didn't actually take her *away*, worse luck! Look here – I said I'd meet you at Venus's temple, didn't I? Well, here I am. I kept my word – did I lie?
Plesidip	Save all that for the court-case. I've heard enough from you. This way! (*Puts a rope round his neck*)
Labrax	Help! Charmides, help! Help me, for pity's sake! I'm being dragged off to court – they've put a rope round my neck!

Charmides, hearing shouts, comes out of the temple.

Charmides	Someone calling me?
Labrax	Look! I'm being manhandled! *Look!*
Charmides	I am looking. Yes, I'm delighted to see it.
Labrax	Aren't you going to help me?
Charmides	Who's that who's got you in tow? 1260
Labrax	Young Plesidippus.
Charmides	Well, he's all yours, Plesidippus. (*To Labrax*) You'd best creep off to jail and put a brave face on it! After all, you've got what most folk only dream of getting!
Labrax	What's that?
Charmides	What they've been asking for!
Labrax	Come along with me, *please*, I'm *begging* you!
Charmides	Just what I'd expect from your sort! You're on your way to jail, and you beg me to come with you! (*To Plesidippus*) Still got him tight, sir?

Plesidippus draws the noose tighter.

Labrax	Aaagh! He's choking me!
Plesidip	I wish I were. Now, Palaestra dear, and Ampelisca, you wait where you are until I get back here.
Turbalio	Better, sir, if they come over to our place, I think –

47

	until you can collect them.	
Plesidip	Very well, that's kind of you.	
Labrax	You – thieves, you!	
Turbalio	Thieves, are we? Off with him!	
Labrax	Help, help! Palaestra, mercy!	1280
Plesidip	This way, scum!	
Labrax	(*to Charmides*) My dear friend...	
Charmides	I'm no friend of yours. I've done with you and your friendship!	
Labrax	You'd throw me over like this?	
Charmides	Yes – just like this. 'Once bitten...'	
Labrax	Well, damn you to hell!	
Charmides	The same to you!	

Labrax goes off. Palaestra, Ampelisca and the two slaves go into the cottage.

It must be true what they say about people changing into different animals: the pimp's changing into a collared dove, I reckon – they'll soon be collaring him, anyway; they'll throw him into prison neck and crop, and he'll be building a jail-bird's nest inside!... But I'll go along to offer him some legal aid – anything to get him ... sentenced more quickly!   1296

Charmides goes off. Daemones comes out of the cottage.

Daemones   That was a good piece of work I did today, helping those two young ladies, and I've found myself a couple of the most attractive protégées into the bargain!... and delightfully young, both of them ... But my wretched wife is watching me like a hawk in case I so much as *look* in their direction! (*Looks out to sea thoughtfully*) I wonder what on earth my slave Gripus is up to. He went to sea to fish last night – heaven knows, he'd have done better to stay in bed at home! There's been such a storm all night and all day, he's just wasting time and good nets! Anything he catches in a swell like this I'll ... fry on my own fingers!... (*Listens*) There's my wife calling me in for lunch. I'm off inside – for another earful of stupid small-talk!

48

Daemones goes in. Gripus comes up from the sea – stage left – dragging a net containing no fish, but a trunk-like object. He is overjoyed.

Gripus To Neptune, dweller in the salt abodes
　　Of fishes in the untrodden sea,
High praise and hearty thanks I give
　　For treatin' me so handsomely!
For Neptune from 'is vast domain
　　Dispatched me 'omeward safe and sound,
Me boat leak-free in a stormy sea,
And *what* a remarkable fish I've found!　　1319
It's a strange sort of monster 'e cast in me net,
But the richest catch *I*'m ever likely to get!
　　I'm weighed down to the ground
　　With the treasure I've found!
　　It's incredibly lucky the way
　　Me fishin' trip turned out today –
Not a scale not a fin did me fishin' bring in,
Just this 'ere – all the rest got away!
I leapt from me bed at the dead of night
　　At the thought of the money I'd make;
I put business before a comfortable snore
　　Fer me and me master's sake.
I'd determined to sail in a force eight gale,
　　Not a thought fer meself I gave,
And by risking disaster earn cash fer me master,
　　– And do a good turn fer 'is slave!　　1335

Yes – a lazy man's not worth a damn! I never could stand lazy people. A man's gotta rise with the lark if 'e wants to keep to schedule with 'is chores. He's worse than useless if 'e waits till 'is master turns 'im out of bed to go to work. People who love their sleep can rest assured – of no money and a load of trouble! Take me – because I've been up and doin' I've found a way to be idle fer the rest of me life! (*He eyes the trunk in his net, then pats it*) This 'ere's what I found in the sea! Whatever's inside, it weighs a good bit. There's gold in there, I bet – and no one knows anything about it but yours truly! Gripus, old friend, you've got the chance to be as free as any man alive! Now 'ere's what I've made up me mind to do: I'll go up to me master, cunning like, and sly, and offer 'im money, bit by bit, until 'e lets me go free. (*Assuming grand airs*) And when I'm free, I'll get meself a bit of land, an 'ouse – slaves, too. I'll 'ave a large fleet of ships and become a merchant. (*Warming to the subject*) I'll be famous, rub shoulders with royalty! Then I'll build meself a yacht – just fer fun, and I'll sail round all the cities of the world like Stratonicus![8]

> And when me greatness spreads abroad
> And me name becomes an 'ousehold word, 1360
> I'll found GRIPOPOLIS the Great –
> A city I shall dedicate
> To immortalise me great career –
> I'll even start an empire there!

Ah yes, you've gotta think *big*!... But now I'd better 'ide this trunk ... Hm, meanwhile, 'is lordship is going to 'ave to breakfast off sour wine and sea-salt – nothin' to go with it, neither!

Enter Trachalio, slave of Plesidippus.

Trachalio	Hey, you, wait a minute!
Gripus	Why should I?
Trachalio	One of your ropes is trailing – let me wind it up for you.
Gripus	Just leave it alone, will you?
Trachalio	I'm only trying to give you a hand. One good turn deserves –
Gripus	Look, if it's fish yer after, sonny, you can forget it. There was a hell of a blow last night, and I 'aven't got a sausage! Can't you see this net I'm bringin' in? Not a sardine in sight!
Trachalio	But I'm not *after* fish. I'd just like a couple of words with you. 1381
Gripus	Well, you're a damn nuisance, whoever you are.

Gripus makes as if to go, but Trachalio holds on to the rope.

Trachalio Not so fast! I'm not letting you rush off like that. Hold on a moment.

Gripus You watch it, fella! What d'you mean, 'anging on to me like this, eh?

Trachalio Listen, and maybe you'll find out.

Gripus I don't *want* to listen.

Trachalio Well, you're going to, whether you like it or not.

Gripus All right, all right, what's on your mind?

Trachalio Now this is going to interest you.

Gripus Why don't you tell me what it is, then?

Trachalio Make sure no one's listening in on us.

Gripus Why? What difference would that make?

Trachalio A lot. Can I trust you to keep a secret?

Gripus (*becoming impatient*) Look. Just tell me what all this is about.

Trachalio I will – all right – if you give me your word you won't breathe a word to anyone else.

Gripus All right, whoever you are, I promise. I'll keep my word.   1401

Trachalio Listen to this, then: I saw a man committing a theft, and I knew the man he was robbing. I went up to the thief and tried to strike a bargain with him. I said: 'I know the man this belongs to, but if you give me half, I'll keep quiet about it.' But he didn't want to know. What *would*'ve been fair, d'you think? Fifty–fifty? I think so, don't you?

Gripus Not *likely*! You should've asked more! If 'e doesn't cough up, you ought to tell the owner.

Trachalio Yes – that's *just* what I'll do… Now listen carefully: because all this concerns – *you*!

Gripus Eh? What've *I* done?

Trachalio That trunk. I know who it belongs to. I've known him for years, in fact.

Gripus *What*'s this?

Trachalio *And* I know how it was lost.   1417

Gripus And *I* know 'ow it was found, *and* I know who found it, *and* I know who owns it now! And that's no concern of yours – any more than your story con-

51

cerns *me*! You may know whose it *used* to be – well, I know whose it is *now*! Nobody's going to take it away from me, so don't think you can try it on!

Trachalio What if the owner came along? Wouldn't you give it back to *him*?

Gripus I *am* the owner, get that into your skull! *I*'m the one who netted this little lot, and nobody else has got any right to it at all.

Trachalio Is that so?

Gripus You wouldn't lay claim to one particular fish in the sea and say 'This one belongs to *me*', would you? Any fish I catch – if I do catch any, that is – are *my* fish. Catchin's keepin'. I regard 'em as me own property, and nobody's ever disputed the fact; nobody comes and demands a percentage! I sell me fish in the market – they're me wares. The sea's common property, that much I *do* know.

Trachalio I agree. Why isn't this trunk as much my property as yours, then? It was fished out of the sea, and you yourself said the sea's common property.   1440

Gripus *You*'ve got a bleedin' cheek! If what you said was law, all us fishermen 'd be lookin' fer jobs! When the fish are put out in the market, nobody'd spend a penny on 'em. They'd all say they were caught in common property and demand their share!

Trachalio It's *you* who've got the nerve! Try to compare trunks with fish, would you? You can't be saying they're the same – surely!

Gripus Same or not, I can't 'elp it. I let down me net and 'ook, and whatever sticks to it I pulls up. What I've caught with me own 'ands is mine, and what's mine's me own!

Trachalio Ah, but it *isn't*. It can't be yours if it's someone else's.

Gripus Oh ho, we're a philosopher, are we?

Trachalio Look, you shyster, have you ever seen a fisherman catch or sell a 'trunkfish'? You can't monopolise all the trades round here! You're posing as a trunk-maker and a fisherman at one and the same time, you blighter! Come on, then: you explain to me

how a trunk can be a fish or else ... you can kiss
that trunk goodbye! I'm not letting you run away
with it. It didn't *belong* in the sea, and it doesn't *look*
as if it did! 1464

Gripus What? Never 'eard of the trunkfish before?

Trachalio It doesn't exist, you damned fool!

Gripus Oh yes it does! I'm a fisherman. *I* ought to know.
'Course, it's not caught that often – very rarely
comes near land, y'see.

Trachalio Oh, rubbish! Don't give me that, you thieving
bastard!

Gripus (*continues unabashed*) ... this one's an unusual
colour, though, I 'as to admit. It's usually the little
fellows come in this shade. Others 'ave reddish
skins, big 'uns, like this one of mine. And sometimes they can be black.

Trachalio Yes, yes, of course. *You*'ll be turning into all kinds
of trunkfish yourself before long, if you don't watch
it! You'll go red, then black and blue... 1479

Gripus (*to himself*) Charming! What *nice* people yer meet!

Trachalio Come on, we're wasting time with all this
talk. Let's find someone to settle the argu-
ment.

Gripus Let the *trunk* settle it!

*Gripus grabs one end of the rope and pulls. Trachalio
hangs on to the other end.*

Trachalio So that's the way you want it, eh?

Gripus (*grunting*) Yeah.

Trachalio (*realising Gripus is stronger*) Oh, you haven't got a
brain in your head!

Gripus Thanks, professor!

Trachalio You're not walking off with that trunk! You name
an arbitrator, a trustee, perhaps – someone who
can settle this once and for all.

Gripus You must be mad!

Trachalio Mad? Yes – I'm positively frothing at the mouth –
so watch it!

Gripus Well, I've got the very devil in me, and I'm *not*

	letting go of this trunk!
Trachalio	One more word from you and I'll bash your brains in! If you don't let go this second, I'll squeeze your innards out like water from a sponge – right to the last drop! 1501
Gripus	Lay one finger on me! I'll dash you to pieces on the ground, like an octopus. Come on then, want to make something of it?
Trachalio	(*backing down*) Er, what's the point? Why not just split the loot?
Gripus	The only split you'll get from me's a split lip. You can forget it, mate. I'm off.
Trachalio	(*grabs rope and pulls Gripus back*) Whoa there, hard astern! Easy as you go, mister!
Gripus	Look, you may think you're the look-out on this 'ere boat, but I'm steerin' it. Leggo that rope, swab!
Trachalio	You let go of the trunk, then.
Gripus	(*changing tack desperately*) You'll never make a brass farthin' out of this lot, you know. Honest!
Trachalio	It's no good trying to put me off it now. Either cut me in, or we'll have to find an arbitrator, or someone to look after it for us.
Gripus	But it's mine, damn it! I fished it out of the sea...
Trachalio	I know; I saw you from the shore. 1520
Gripus	... caught it by me own skill and 'ard work, in me own net, workin' in me own boat!
Trachalio	Ah, but if the owner came along now, I should be just as guilty as you are. *You* may be the thief, but I *witnessed* the theft. Right?
Gripus	(*not thinking very hard*) Right.
Trachalio	Hold on, then, you swindling scum, if I was in on the *theft*, why aren't I in on the *proceeds*, eh? Tell me *that*!
Gripus	Damme if I know. I don't understand this legal clap-trap at all. One thing I *do* know is – this trunk's *mine*!
Trachalio	And I say it's *mine*.
Gripus	(*hitting on a new idea*) Hold on, I've *got* it! I've thought of a way you can avoid being accused either as a thief *or* as a witness!

54

Trachalio How?

Gripus Just let *me* go my way, and *you* keep your trap shut and go *yours*! You tell nobody about me, and I won't give you any of the loot. You keep quiet about *me*, and I'll keep quiet about *you*. Yes, that's the most sensible solution! 1542

Trachalio (*impatiently*) Look, are you going to make me a decent offer or not?

Gripus I *have* been, for some time now: you clear off, let go of the rope and don't bother me again!

Trachalio Just a minute, I'm making you a *counter*-offer.

Gripus Oh, *push* offer, will yer?

Trachalio Do you know anyone round here?

Gripus They're my neighbours, I *should* do!

Trachalio Where do you live then?

Gripus (*hedging*) Oh, er ... *way* over there ... right over the fields, as far as you can see.

Trachalio Well, why don't we leave the matter in the hands of whoever lives in this cottage? All right?

Gripus Slacken off the rope while I chew it over a minute.

Trachalio All right.

Gripus (*aside*) Must be my lucky day! It's as good as buttoned up now! The trunk's mine fer good! 'e's only goin' to ask me master to arbitrate! We're right in me own back garden! The fool doesn't know what 'e's doin'! Me master won't part with a penny piece! I'll take 'im up on it. 1563

Trachalio Well, what do you say?

Gripus I know damn well the trunk's mine be rights, but rather than fight yer for it, I'll go along with yer.

Trachalio Now you're being reasonable.

Gripus I've no idea who this arbitrator is you're takin' me to, but if 'e's straight, 'e'll be a friend right away, even if I never set eyes on 'im before. But if 'e's bent, even if I know 'im, 'e'll never be a friend of *mine* again!

Daemones comes out of the cottage again with Palaestra and Ampelisca. The two slaves follow.

Daemones Look here, my dears, I promise you – I'd willingly

55

do anything I can to help, but I'm afraid my wife will throw me out of the house because of you – she'll say I've flaunted two young fancy pieces right under her nose! So off to the altar with you both – it's either you or me, and I'd rather it was you!

Palaestra } **Ampelisca** }	Oh dear! What shall we do now? 1579
Daemones	Don't worry, I'll see you come to no harm. (*Turns and sees the two slaves*) Why are *you* following me out here? No one will do them any harm while I'm here! Go back into the house, go on! Your duty's done. Dismiss!

The two slaves go back into the cottage.

Gripus	'Morning, master.
Daemones	Good morning, Gripus! Any luck?

Daemones moves over to Gripus. Palaestra and Ampelisca go to the altar.

Trachalio	(*astonished*) Is this – *your* slave?
Gripus	And proud of it, yes!
Trachalio	I wasn't talking to you.
Gripus	Well, push off, then.
Trachalio	(*to Daemones*) If you'd kindly give me an answer, sir: is this *your* slave?
Daemones	He is.
Trachalio	Oh, well, that's *fine* then, if he is, just fine! Let me wish you another good morning!
Daemones	The same to you. Aren't you the man who went off to fetch his master a while back?
Trachalio	That's me, yes.
Daemones	What do you want now?
Trachalio	Is this chap *really* your slave? 1600
Daemones	He is, yes.
Trachalio	Well, that's fine, then, if he is. *Fine!*
Daemones	What are you going on about?
Trachalio	The man's a *criminal*!
Daemones	What crime has he committed against you?
Trachalio	I'd like to see both his legs broken!

Daemones	What *is* all this? What's the quarrel between you two?
Trachalio	I'll tell you –
Gripus	No, *I*'ll tell him.
Trachalio	The honour's *mine*, I believe – I'm the plaintiff.
Gripus	If you 'ad any sense of decency, you'd honour us by shoving off!
Daemones	Gripus, shut up and listen!
Gripus	What? Let 'im get in first?
Daemones	Yes. Just listen. (*To Trachalio*) Go on, then.
Gripus	You'd listen to someone else before your own slave? *Well!*
Trachalio	No stopping this fellow, is there! Well, as I was about to say ... you remember that pimp you kicked out of the temple a while back – this fellow's got his trunk. Look! 1622
Gripus	I 'ave *not!*
Trachalio	How can you deny it – think I'm *blind*?
Gripus	(*aside*) I wish you were! (*Aloud*) Whether I've got it or I 'aven't got it – what's it to you *what* I do?
Trachalio	The important question is *how* you got it – legally or *ill*egally.
Gripus	(*to Daemones*) Look, I fished this up out of the sea, sir, you can crucify me if I didn't! (*To Trachalio*) If I pulled this up in me net, 'ow come it's yours not mine, eh?
Trachalio	(*to Daemones*) He's just prevaricating. The facts are exactly as I've stated them.
Gripus	Eh? What's that?
Trachalio	*I*'m supposed to be speaking first, I think. (*To Daemones*) If this fellow's yours, then *stop* him!
Gripus	Eh? We don't *all* get up to that sort of thing, you know. *You* may be like that, but my master's not! 1640
Daemones	(*laughing*) One up to Gripus! Now, what is it you want, tell me.
Trachalio	I'm not claiming anything in that trunk for myself, and I never said it was mine. But there's a little box inside that belongs to one of the girls here, the one I told you earlier was free.

57

Daemones	You mean the one you said was a compatriot of mine?
Trachalio	That's the one – and the keepsakes she carried about when she was young are in the little box that's inside the trunk. Now they're no earthly use to him, and he'll be helping the poor girl out if he gives them back, because they're the only way she can find her parents again.
Daemones	I'll certainly see he gives them to her. (*To Gripus*) Keep quiet, you!
Gripus	Damn me if I'm giving anything to him!
Trachalio	Look, I only want the little box and the trinkets inside.
Gripus	What if they're gold? 1660
Trachalio	What if they are? We'll give you their value, gold for gold, silver for silver.
Gripus	Show me your gold first – *then* I'll let you see the box.
Daemones	(*to Gripus*) You keep quiet and watch your step! (*To Trachalio*) Go on.
Trachalio	All I ask is that you take pity on the girl, sir, if this really is the pimp's trunk – as I suspect. I can't say it is for certain yet, you see; I'm guessing.
Gripus	*See?* The blighter's only fishin'!
Trachalio	Let me go on. If this is the old rogue's trunk, as I say, the girls will be able to recognise it. Make him show it to them.
Gripus	Eh? *Show* it to them?
Daemones	That's fair enough, Gripus – just showing it to them.
Gripus	No it's not, by God; it's damned *un*fair!
Daemones	Why?
Gripus	Because once I show it 'em, they'll obviously say straight off they recognise it. 1680
Trachalio	You low-down crook – you expect everyone to be just like you, do you?
Gripus	Call me what you like, I don't care, so long as me master stands by me!
Trachalio	He may stand by you now – but where will he stand when he hears evidence from *this* side?

58

Daemones	(*to Gripus*) Just *listen*, Gripus! (*To Trachalio*) Tell me briefly what you want.
Trachalio	I've told you, but I'll tell you again if you didn't understand the first time. These two girls, as I said, ought to be free. Palaestra here was kidnapped from Athens as a baby.
Gripus	What's it gotta do with the trunk – tell me – whether they're free or not?
Trachalio	I suppose you want me to say *everything* twice, do you, you blighter, just to waste time?
Daemones	Cut out the insults and just answer my question.
Trachalio	There should be a little wooden box in that trunk, and it contains the things which will help her find her parents. She had them with her when she was kidnapped as a baby – from Athens – as I said before. 1702
Gripus	God damn yer, man, you and yer poisonous tongue – what are you still yappin' for? These girls aren't dumb, are they? Can't they speak fer themselves?
Trachalio	Women are best seen and not heard.
Gripus	Well, *you* don't count as a man *or* a woman.
Trachalio	What d'you mean?
Gripus	You're useless on both counts, whether you're talking or not! (*To Daemones*) Now, am I *ever* going to get the chance to speak?
Daemones	Speak one word from now on and I'll brain you!
Trachalio	As I was saying, sir – *please* will you get him to give the box back to the girls? If he wants a reward for it, he shall have it. And he can keep anything else that's inside the box.
Gripus	Ah, you're saying that now because you know it's mine by rights. Just now you were asking for half of it.
Trachalio	I still am!
Gripus	Oh yes? I've seen kites looking for a kill and getting nothing, you know! 1721
Daemones	Do I have to have you thrashed to shut you up?
Gripus	If he shuts up, *I*'ll shut up; if *he* speaks, let *me* speak too.
Daemones	Give me that trunk, Gripus.
Gripus	All right, I'll give it to you – but only if you give it

	back if the box isn't inside.
Daemones	You'll get it back.
Gripus	There.
Daemones	Now, Palaestra and Ampelisca, both of you listen to what I say: is this the trunk you said your box was in?
Palaestra	That's the one, yes!
Gripus	Hell, wouldn't it *just* be! One look and she says it's hers!
Palaestra	(*to Daemones*) I can prove it to you easily. Inside the trunk there should be a little wooden box, and I'll tell you what's inside it, article by article. Don't show me any of it – and if I make a single mistake, forget what I say and keep it all for yourselves. But if I'm right, then please will you let me have my things back?

1742

Daemones	Agreed, yes. That all seems fair enough if you ask me.
Gripus	Bloody *un*fair, if you ask me! What if she's a clairvoyante or a fortune-teller or something, and she can just run through everything that's in there? You going to 'and it all over to a fortune-teller?
Daemones	She'll only have it if she gets every detail right: fortune-telling won't do her any good. Unfasten that trunk, so I can see what's in it once and for all.
Trachalio	(*triumphantly*) So much for Gripus!
Gripus	There we are – undone.
Daemones	Open it right up.
	Gripus lifts the lid.
	I can see a little box.
	(*Holds it up*)
	Is this the one?
Palaestra	Yes, that's it! . . . Oh, my dear, dear parents, all I have of you is inside this box! All my hopes of finding you I kept in there!
Gripus	Then you deserve everything the gods send you, whoever you are – shutting up your mum and dad in such a tiny box!

1762

Daemones	Gripus, you come here – it's you who are on trial. Palaestra, you keep your distance; stand over there,

and tell me what's inside and describe each thing in detail. If you make the tiniest mistake and think you can change it later, you've another think coming, my girl!

Gripus   That's fair enough.

Trachalio He's not asking *you*, dammit – *you*'re the one in the wrong!

Daemones   (*opening the box*) Now then, young lady, speak up! Gripus, pay attention and keep quiet!

Palaestra There's a necklace of lucky charms.

Daemones   Here it is!

Gripus   Finished in the first round! (*To Daemones*) Hey, don't *show* it to her!

Daemones   What sort of charms? Tell me what they are in the right order.   1779

Palaestra There's a little gold sword with an inscription on it.

Daemones   And what is the inscription on the little sword?

Palaestra The name of my father. Then, on the other side, there's a little two-headed axe – that's gold, too – and that has my mother's name on it.

Daemones   Just a moment! What is the name on the sword – your father's name?

Palaestra Daemones.

Daemones   Gods above! Can I dare hope – ?

Gripus   (*agitated*) Damn you – can *I*?

Trachalio (*to Daemones and Palaestra*) Keep going, for heaven's sake!

Gripus   (*to Trachalio*) Ease up, damn you!

Daemones   Tell me your mother's name, on the little axe.

Palaestra Daedalis.

Daemones   Then heaven *is* on my side!

Gripus   Not on mine, though.

Daemones   Gripus, this must be my own daughter!

Gripus   All right, all right, she's your daughter (*To Trachalio*) As fer you, I 'ope you rot in 'ell for ever setting *eyes* on me today – me too, idiot that I was not to look about and make sure no one was spying on me before I pulled that net out of the water!   1802

Palaestra (*continuing*) Then there's a little silver sickle and a tiny pair of clasped hands and a little pig –

Gripus   Oh, get *lost*, won't you? – and take all your perishing piglets with you!

Palaestra And there's a gold locket my father gave me on my birthday.

Daemones   It's here, it really is! Oh, I can't wait to hold her in my arms any longer! My dear girl, my own daughter! I am your father, I was the one who brought you up – Daemones! Your mother Daedalis is inside the cottage!

Palaestra Oh! *Father!* The father I had given up all hope of finding!

Daemones   My *dear*! How *happy* I am to hold you in my arms!

Trachalio This is splendid! How good it is to see this happening to two such deserving people!

Daemones   Come on, Trachalio – take this trunk, if you can manage, and put it indoors.   1820

Trachalio Look at poor old Gripus now! Gripus, your hard luck really makes me ... glad!

Daemones   Let's go inside to see your mother, my child. She'll be able to get together with you and find out exactly what happened – she had more to do with you, she knew more about all those trinkets and toys of yours.

Trachalio Let's *all* go in – we've all had a part in this.

Palaestra This way, Ampelisca, come on!

Ampelisca I'm *so* pleased at the way things have turned out for you!

Daemones, Trachalio, Palaestra and Ampelisca go into the cottage.

Gripus   What a damn fool I was to fish up that trunk today! Or rather, when I'd fished it up, for not thinking to hide it somewhere out of the way! And I really thought I'd have a wild time with a catch like that, bein' as how it came from such a wild, stormy sea! I'm damned *sure* it's stuffed with gold and silver, too! Oh hell, I might as well go off inside, find somewhere quiet and hang myself – at least for a while, till I stop feeling so bloody *sore* about everything!   1841

Gripus goes in. Daemones comes out again.

Daemones   Ye Gods above!
Is there a luckier man on earth than I?
To find my long-lost daughter – just like that!
But there it is: if once the gods decide
A man is worth a helping hand, they find
A way of answering his prayers somehow.
This is a thing I never really hoped
Nor ever *thought* could happen – yet it did!
Out of the blue I've found my girl again!
I'm going to marry her to a fine young man,
A citizen of Athens, well-connected, well,
A relative of mine, in fact!   1853

Yes, I must have him brought here as soon as possible. (*Looks about*) Now where is that slave of his?
I've already told him to come out because I want
him to go over to the market place for me. I wonder
why he's not here yet. I suppose I'll have to go and
see for myself. (*Goes to the door*) What's all this? Oh
Lord, my wife, arms wrapped round Palaestra's
neck, hugging her to death! Really, taking it all *this*
far gets a bit sickening! (*Calls inside*) You'll have to
stop all that kissing some time, woman! And get
things ready for me to make an offering to the
household gods when I come back in; after all,
they've made an addition to our family! We've
some lambs and pigs for sacrifice inside. Hullo?
You women, what *are* you doing with Trachalio in
there? . . . Ah, good, here he comes now.

Trachalio comes on.

Trachalio   (*eagerly*) Wherever he is, I'll find him – *wherever* he
is, I'll bring Plesidippus back with me.
Daemones   Tell him what's happened about my daughter. Ask
him to drop everything else and come here.
Trachalio   Right.
Daemones   Say I'll let him marry my daughter.

Trachalio	Right.
Daemones	Say I know his father and I'm related to him, in fact.
Trachalio	Right.
Daemones	And *hurry*! 1880
Trachalio	Right.
Daemones	Get him here soon, so we can see to the dinner.
Trachalio	Right.
Daemones	Got all that all right?
Trachalio	Right enough, yes... Oh, there's something you can do for me... You promised I should be free today – remember?
Daemones	Right.
Trachalio	Don't forget to ask Plesidippus to set me free, then.
Daemones	Right.
Trachalio	Have your daughter ask him, too – she'll get whatever she wants from him!
Daemones	Right.
Trachalio	And when I'm free I want Ampelisca as my wife.
Daemones	Right.
Trachalio	*And* I want a decent reward for services rendered.
Daemones	Right.
Trachalio	Got all that all right?
Daemones	(*becoming impatient*) Right enough, yes... And that, I think, about evens the score! Now off with you to the city and get back here as soon as you can.
Trachalio	All *right*! I'll be *right* back! (*Cheekily*) See to everything here while I'm gone, will you? 1903
Daemones	*All right!*
	Trachalio goes off.
	Right, right, 'right' to everything I said, damn him! My ears are ringing with 'rights'! Well, I hope it's *last rites* for him!

Gripus enters from the cottage.

Gripus	Is it all right (*Daemones starts at the word*) if I 'ave a word with you, sir?
Daemones	Eh? Oh, what's the matter, Gripus?
Gripus	About that trunk, sir. Er, if you 'ad any sense you'd

64

er ... show you 'ad some sense – you'd 'ang on to what the gods 'ave blessed you with!

Daemones Do you think it right for me to call what is someone else's property *mine*?

Gripus What? Something I found in the sea?

Daemones All the luckier for the man who lost it, I say! It's no reason for the trunk to change owners!

Gripus That's why you're so hard up – you're too damned *honest*! 1920

Daemones (*waxing lyrical*)

Oh, Gripus, Gripus, in our lives there are
So many snares to catch the unwary out!
And many of these snares are baited, too,
And if you seize the bait too greedily
You're caught – ensnared by your own avarice!
The prudent, thoughtful man who acts with care,
Can long enjoy his honestly-won wealth;
But ill-won wealth like yours, I think,
Will soon change hands! Better to let it go
Than keep it, and face even greater loss!
Shall I receive what has been brought to me
Knowing it is another's, and conceal the fact?
No, *never*; never shall I behave like that.
Not Daemones! The wisest masters take good care
Never to act as party to their servants' crimes.
Me? I've no time for crooked partnerships –
Nor all the crooked wealth that they produce!

Gripus (*appalled*) *Blimey*, I've 'eard actors goin' on like that before now – spouting all those words of wisdom, and gettin' a good round of applause, too – preachin' to the people about 'ow to behave. But when they went off 'ome afterwards, I don't remember any of 'em takin' a blind bit of notice of what they'd said! 1944

Daemones Off you go inside, now, before you really annoy me! And just watch your tongue! I'm not giving you a thing, so get *that* into your head!

Gripus Well, I just 'ope and pray that whatever's inside that trunk – gold or silver or whatever – turns to dust and ashes!

RUDENS

Gripus goes in.

Daemones   There you are now – that's just how our slaves get corrupted. If he'd met another slave they'd have agreed to be in on the theft together. He'd have thought he'd netted a really splendid catch – and all the time he'd have been caught himself – led captive by what he'd captured, in fact! (*Laughs at his joke*) ... Well, now I'm off to make sacrifice; as soon as that's done, I'll have the dinner prepared.

Daemones goes into the cottage. Plesidippus comes on from the town with Trachalio.

Plesidip   Once again, now – go over it all once again, Trachalio, my dear boy, – my freedman, no, my *benefactor*, no, no, my very *father*! Has Palaestra *really* found her father and mother?   1962

Trachalio   She has, really!

Plesidip   And she's an Athenian, same as me?

Trachalio   I believe so.

Plesidip   And she's going to marry me?

Trachalio   I expect so.

Plesidip   Do you reckon she'll be mine today?

Trachalio   I reckon so.

Plesidip   Do you reckon I should congratulate her father on finding her?

Trachalio   I reckon so.

Plesidip   And her mother, d'you reckon?

Trachalio   I reckon so.

Plesidip   (*playfully*) *What* do you reckon, though?

Trachalio   Whatever you say, I reckon!

Plesidip   How *much* do you reckon it at?

Trachalio   Eh? Don't ask me. I just reckon, that's all!

Plesidip   Well, stop it! I'm here – you've *me* to reckon with now!   1980

Trachalio   I reckon so.

Plesidip   Should I run inside, d'you reckon?

Trachalio   I reckon so.

Plesidip   Or go in more ... calmly, like this?

Trachalio   I reckon so.

66

Plesidip   Should I greet her too as I go in?
Trachalio   I reckon so.
Plesidip   Her father as well?
Trachalio   I reckon so.
Plesidip   *After* her mother?
Trachalio   I reckon so.
Plesidip   *Then* what? When I go in, should I throw my arms round her father?
Trachalio   Eh? No, I reckon *not!*
Plesidip   What about her mother?
Trachalio   No, I reckon not.
Plesidip   What about Palaestra herself?
Trachalio   No, I reckon not.
Plesidip   *Damnation!* He's come to the end of his reckoning. Now I want him to reckon Yes, he reckons No!
Trachalio   You're daft! Come on!   2001
Plesidip   Trachalio, my champion, lead me wherever you please!

Plesidippus and Trachalio go into the cottage. Meanwhile, Labrax, having lost his case in court, comes back feeling very sorry for himself.

Labrax   There can't be a man alive more miserable than I am! Plesidippus has just had me in front of the magistrates and won his case, and I've been sentenced to lose Palaestra! I'm *finished!* It must be true what they say about pimps being the 'sons of joy' – at any rate, whenever a pimp's up against it, everybody seems highly delighted!... Now I'm going to go and see that other girl of mine in the temple of Venus here. She's all that's left of what I had, and I'm going to make off with her if *nothing* else!

Gripus enters from the cottage in a surly mood. Labrax observes him for a while.

Gripus   If I don't get that trunk back by this evening, I'll be a goner, I swear it! You'll have seen the last of Gripus!
Labrax   Eh? *Trunk?* God, just to hear the word is torture –

67

	it's agony, like a stake being stuck in my stomach!
Gripus	That bastard Trachalio's a free man – and look at me! Not a sausage for the one who caught the trunk and fished it out the sea in 'is net – not a thing!
Labrax	Ye Gods! Now he really *has* got me interested! 2022
Gripus	I'm going to stick up an advertisement everywhere in letters two feet 'igh: 'ANYONE LOSING A TRUNK STUFFED WITH GOLD AND SILVER SHOULD CONTACT GRIPUS.' *You* lot aren't 'aving it, if you think you are! *Oh* no!
Labrax	Lord, this fellow knows who's got my trunk, unless I'm mistaken! I must have a word with him. May the gods be on my side!
Gripus	(*answering a call from inside*) What do you want me in there for? I just want to clean this spit outside the front door. It's more rust than iron, this spit – the more I clean it the redder and thinner it gets! It's not normal, if you ask me: it falls apart as soon as I touch it!
Labrax	Good day, young fellow!
Gripus	Hullo to you too, hairy!
Labrax	How're things with you?
Gripus	All spit and polish! 2040
Labrax	How are you? Well, I hope?
Gripus	You in the medical business, then?
Labrax	Er – no, not exactly.
Gripus	(*surveying him*) Ah … out of business altogether, are you?
Labrax	(*wincing*) You got it in one!
Gripus	I must say you look the part! What's up?
Labrax	Last night I was shipwrecked – me and my friend – and I lost everything I had in the world.
Gripus	What exactly was that?
Labrax	A trunk full of gold and silver.
Gripus	Er … can you remember what was in that trunk you lost?
Labrax	What does it matter? – it's lost!
Gripus	But –
Labrax	Oh, leave it! Let's talk about something else.
Gripus	What if I knew the bloke as found it? You'll 'ave to

give me some means of identification, of course.

Labrax   There are eight hundred gold pieces in a wallet, and a hundred gold sovereigns besides in a leather bag.   2061

Gripus   (*aside*) Wow! That's a lot of loot! I'll get a big reward for this! Well, well, there's *some* justice in the world, then – I'll be loaded after all! The trunk's obviously his. (*To Labrax*) Go on, tell me more.

Labrax   A whole talent of good silver – the real stuff, full weight – in a purse, and a bowl, a goblet, a pitcher, an urn and a ladle.

Gripus   Whew! You 'ad a fair old bit, didn't you!

Labrax   'Had', yes, 'had' – that's the crying shame of it – not any more!

Gripus   What would you be prepared to give a chap fer tracking it down and supplying you with information about it? Come on, quick now, quote your figure!

Labrax   Three hundred pieces?

Gripus   Piffle!

Labrax   Four hundred.

Gripus   Rubbish!   2080

Labrax   Five hundred.

Gripus   Chicken feed!

Labrax   *Six* hundred.

Gripus   Peanuts! – the smallest sort!

Labrax   Seven hundred, then.

Gripus   Hot air! Yer wastin' yer breath!

Labrax   I'll make it a thousand.

Gripus   You must be dreaming!

Labrax   That's as far as I go.

Gripus   All right – so long!

Labrax   Listen! If I go – er – you won't get another chance! – *Eleven* hundred.

Gripus   You're joking!

Labrax   Look – you tell me how much you want.

Gripus   Well, I wouldn't want there to be any hard feelings – two thousand would do it. But not a farthing less! Yes or no?

Labrax	Oh, well... I don't have any choice... All right. Two thousand.
Gripus	Come over here. I want Venus to witness it! 2100
Labrax	Yes, yes, whatever you want.
Gripus	Lay your hand on the altar.
Labrax	All right.
Gripus	Swear by Venus.
Labrax	Swear what?
Gripus	What I tell you.
Labrax	Go on, then, whatever you like. (*Aside*) Swearing's easy enough – I don't need any help with *this*!
Gripus	Lay hold of the altar.
Labrax	Right.
Gripus	Swear you'll give me the money on the same day you get the trunk.
Labrax	Very good.
Gripus	'Venus of Cyrene, be my witness, if I find the trunk I lost at sea, with all the gold and silver intact, and it returns to my possession, then I will give this man Gripus' – say so, and touch me as you say it –
Labrax	'... then I will give this man Gripus – hear that Venus? – two thousand pieces – no questions.'
Gripus	And pray, if you do the dirty on me, that Venus smash you to smithereens, dash you to damnation, you and all yer pimpery! (*Aside*) Which I 'ope 'appens anyway, whether you keep yer oath or not!
Labrax	All right. 'If I break this oath in any way, Venus, you can damn the whole pimping profession.' 2125
Gripus	(*aside*) They'll be damned, all right, whether you keep yer word or not! (*To Labrax*) You wait here and I'll get the old man to come out. You ask him for yer trunk straight out.

Gripus goes in.

Labrax	Even if he does give that trunk back, I'm not paying him a penny piece, damn me if I do! My tongue can swear all it likes – but I'll do as I please! (*Turns*) Sh! Here he comes with the old man.

Gripus re-enters with Daemones.

Gripus	This way.
Daemones	Where is that pimp?
Gripus	(*to Labrax*) Hey, you! Here we are! (*Points to Daemones*) He's got the trunk.
Daemones	Yes, I have – I admit it. I've got it at home. If it's really yours, you can have it.
	Signals to Gripus, who goes to fetch it.
	You'll find it all safe and sound, everything that was inside. 2141
	Gripus returns.
	Take it, if it's yours.
Labrax	Gods above, it *is* mine, too! Welcome back, my old friend!
Gripus	*Is* it yours?
Labrax	Is it mine? (*Grabs it*) Look, if it was Jove Almighty's, I couldn't care less – it's *mine now*!
Daemones	It's all there, safe and sound – except for one small box I took out, a box of trinkets – and with the help of those trinkets I've been able to find my long-lost daughter again!
Labrax	Eh? What daughter?
Daemones	The girl you called Palaestra who used to work for you – she has turned out to be my daughter!
Labrax	(*stunned*) Oh, splendid, marvellous … yes … what extraordinary luck … er … I'm so glad for you!
Daemones	Hm, glad, are you? I can't say I'm entirely convinced.
Labrax	No, no, I am glad, really, I promise – you keep her – I'll give her to you as a present. I won't take a penny piece! 2161
Daemones	Goodness me, what generosity!
Labrax	No, no – you're the generous one! (*Makes as if to go*)
Gripus	(*going over to Labrax*) Hey, you! You got your trunk, then.
Labrax	So?
Gripus	Well, come on then!
Labrax	Come on what?
Gripus	Pay me my money!
Labrax	I'm not paying you a thing. I don't owe you anything!

Gripus	Hullo? What's this? You don't owe me anything?
Labrax	Not a sausage.
Gripus	Didn't you swear an oath to me?
Labrax	Oh, yes, I swore an oath, and I'll swear another if it suits me! Oaths were invented for keeping property, not losing it!
Gripus	Hand over that two thousand in silver, you cheatin' bastard!
Daemones	(*overhearing*) What money is that you're asking for, Gripus? 2181
Gripus	Money he swore to pay me, that's what.
Labrax	Swearing's a hobby of mine. Who made *you* God Almighty if I break the odd oath?
Daemones	Why did he promise you the money?
Gripus	He swore he'd give me two thousand if I delivered his trunk back to him.
Labrax	Right, name your man, and we'll let *him* decide this – we'll soon see if you made a crooked deal or not – *and*, of course, can you be sure I'm not a minor?[9]
Gripus	You deal with 'im. (*Gestures at Daemones*)
Labrax	No, it'll have to be someone else – even if I won my case I'd never get my trunk back from *him*.
Daemones	*Did* you promise him the money?
Labrax	Yes, I admit it.
Daemones	Well, whatever you promised my slave is legally mine – so don't think you can pimp your way out of that one, because you pimping well can't! 2199
Gripus	Thought you'd found someone you could bamboozle, did you? Not on your life! You'll 'ave to cough up – good money, too! And first thing I'm going to do is to give it to 'im (*nods at Daemones*) and buy my freedom.
Daemones	(*to Labrax*) Now, since I've treated you so decently – since it's me you can thank for the return of all this stuff...
Gripus	Eh? I like *that*! *Me*, not *you*!
Daemones	(*to Gripus*) Shut up, you, if you know what's good for you. (*To Labrax*) ... you should show me your gratitude in return, I reckon, by repaying me for all

72

	I've done with a ... reciprocal act of generosity.
Labrax	Ah – so that means you do recognise my rights, then?
Daemones	(*sarcastically*) Your rights? Thank your lucky stars I don't insist on mine!
Gripus	Saved! The pimp's weakening! Freedom, here I come!
Daemones	This fellow found your trunk, and he's my slave. I kept it safe for you, with all the money inside. 2220
Labrax	I'm very grateful to you, and there's no reason why you shouldn't have the two thousand I promised him.
Gripus	Hang on! You give it to *me*, or I'll –
Daemones	Will you keep *quiet*?
Gripus	You're just pretending to side with me – and all the time you're featherin' yer own nest! You're not going to swindle me out of that money, even if I 'ave lost the trunk!
Daemones	One more word from you and I'll have you flogged!
Gripus	You can bloody well *kill* me! But it's going to take two thousand pieces to keep me quiet!
Labrax	(*to Gripus*) Look, pipe down! He's looking after you all right!
Daemones	(*withdrawing*) Come over here, pimp.
Labrax	All right. (*He follows Daemones*)
Gripus	Hey, speak up, come on – I don't like this mumbling and whispering!
Daemones	Tell me, how much did you pay for that other girl – Ampelisca? 2240
Labrax	A thousand.
Daemones	Do you want me to make you a handsome offer?
Labrax	Go on, then.
Daemones	I'll split the two thousand.
Labrax	Now you're talking.
Daemones	You take half for the girl's freedom, and you give me the other half.
Labrax	Fair enough, right.
Daemones	In exchange for that I'll set Gripus free – after all, it was due to him you found your trunk and I found my daughter.

73

Labrax	Very good, I'm much obliged.
Gripus	How soon do I get the money, then?
Daemones	It's all fixed, Gripus. I've got the money.
Gripus	But dammit, I want the money *myself*!
Daemones	Dammit man, there isn't any *for* you, so forget it! I want you to let the pimp off his oath.
Gripus	Oh *hell*, that really is the last straw! I'll do myself in, sure as I live! Damn me if I ever let you swindle me again!

2260

Daemones	Have supper with me tonight, pimp.
Labrax	Splendid – delighted, yes!
Daemones	This way then. (*Turns to audience*) Ladies and gentlemen, I'd invite all of you to dinner, too – if I had anything to offer you – but there's nothing at home worth having! Anyway, I'm sure you all have other invitations! But if you give our play a really *generous* round of applause, you can all come to my place and make a party of it – in er, sixteen years' time! (*To Labrax and Gripus*) You two join me for supper now.
Labrax ⎫ **Gripus** ⎭	We will.
Daemones	Friends – your applause!

NOTES TO RUDENS

1 Arcturus rises in September and sets in November; its rising and setting were thought to bring stormy weather.

2 The *mina*, a Greek weight in silver, was worth 100 *drachmas*, and 60 *minas* made up a talent. No translation of the term is satisfactory today. In another play, the price of a house is 40 *minas*, so Palaestra is far from cheap.

3 An obscure reference to some lost myth.

4 In mythology, Thyestes and Tereus were tricked into eating their own children.

5 This passage is far from certain. In mythology, Philomela

became a nightingale, and her sister Procne, a swallow; they were daughters of Pandion, king of Athens.

6 Silphium was a plant grown around Cyrene whose juice was much prized as a drug and a spice.

7 Vulcan, the god of fire, was married to Venus, who had a love affair with Mars.

8 Stratonicus was a famous travelling musician in the time of Alexander the Great.

9 Gripus was a slave and could not act for himself. Also, a man had to be at least 25 years of age before he could make a legal contract.

Curculio

The scene of *Curculio* is laid at Epidaurus in Argos (East Peloponnese), and the story concerns the love of the hard-up Phaedromus for Planesium, a girl (like Palaestra in *Rudens*) who is in the clutches of a pimp, Cappadox. She is 'promised' to Phaedromus, but actually is about to be bought by a soldier, Therapontigonus, who has already deposited the money for her purchase with a banker. The hero of the piece is Phaedromus's parasite Curculio, who gives the play its name. In Latin *curculio* means 'weevil', an insect found in sacks and granaries that eats many times its own weight of corn. A parasite basically lives by his wits and eats at other people's expense; he generally loves food, especially in quantity, and is willing to be insulted or ridiculed, to flatter or run errands, in order to get it.

Curculio steals the soldier's signet ring, forges a letter and seals it with the ring, and is thus able to get the girl from the pimp for his master. The soldier learns of this and is understandably furious, but the surprising discovery that Planesium is in reality his sister ensures a happy ending.

The plot is therefore a simple one: Phaedromus is in a fix, and his parasite comes to the rescue. Danger arises in the form of the soldier, but the recognition dispels it. Deception and recognition – two vital elements in Plautine plot construction – are cleverly combined, for Therapontigonus's ring both wins the girl for Phaedromus and also reveals her true identity to her brother.

Curculio parades a large number of conventional comic characters – the young impecunious lover, the cheeky slave, the pimp, the parasite, the banker, the cook, the drunken old doorkeeper, the swaggering military type – but they are all freshly and originally drawn. Parasites occur in several of the plays, and have a long tradition in the Greek theatre. The swaggering soldier was another favourite type: later examples of this character are Falstaff (Shakespeare), Ralph Roister Doister (Udall), and Bobadill (Jonson).

Unlike *Rudens* and *Casina*, *Curculio* has no prologue; the unfolding of the plot occurs naturally by means of the dialogue, which is perhaps more acceptable to the modern reader, who often finds the expository prologue something of an embarrassment. (Note, however, that the audience does not learn that the play is set in Epidaurus until as late as line 614.)

There are two other interesting features in this play: first, Phaedromus's serenade to his mistress's door (called a *paraclausithyron*: this is the earliest example in Latin literature) at lines 264 ff.; and secondly, the unusual intervention of the Stage Manager at lines 789 ff., doubtless to 'fill in' while time is supposed to be elapsing off-stage – a function which in older comedy would have been fulfilled by the Chorus.

The Greek original of *Curculio* is unknown; scholars usually place it in the 'middle period' of Plautus. It is short, and made up of conventional elements, but there is a great deal of excellent, fast-moving comedy, and the whole play is a vehicle for the inventive ingenuity of Curculio. So completely does the parasite dominate the scene after his entry at line 501 that we quite forget Palinurus, who was fleshed out rather well in the opening scenes, but never reappears. Perhaps, if Roman acting companies were only five or six strong, as seems likely, he came on again to play the part of Lyco, or Therapontigonus.

Curculio

CHARACTERS

Palinurus	A slave of Phaedromus
Phaedromus	A young man in love with Planesium
Leaena	An old servant woman of Cappadox
Planesium	Phaedromus's sweetheart, finally recognised as the sister of Therapontigonus
Cappadox	Pimp who owns Planesium
Cook	
Curculio	Phaedromus's parasite
Lyco	A banker
Choragus or	
Stage Property Manager	
Therapontigonus	A soldier, discovered to be Planesium's brother

The scene is set in Epidaurus, in a street in front of the homes of Cappadox and Phaedromus, and a temple of Aesculapius, God of Healing. It is night time. The slave Palinurus and his young master Phaedromus enter, carrying torches. They are followed by some slaves.

Palinurus Where on earth are you going at this time of night, Phaedromus, sir – all got up like that, and with this crowd of slaves following you?

Phaedromus (*ecstatic*) Going? Where Venus and Cupid command, where Love lures me, that's where! Midnight, early evening – even if it's a day I have to appear in court, it makes no difference at all. I've no choice in the matter.

Palinurus (*disapproving*) But really, sir, really – !

Phaedromus Really, you're being a *bore*!

Palinurus But sir, this is hardly the thing for a young gentle-

	man like you! Do you want people to know you do all your own dirty work – that you carry your own torch about?	
Phaedromus	(*in a trance*) Torch? This torch is made of wax, wax made by bees – by darling little honey bees! What better to be taking to my own little darling?	
Palinurus	Where are you going, then?	
Phaedromus	(*coyly*) Ask me, and I'll tell you.	
Palinurus	I am asking you – so tell me. Well?	20
Phaedromus	(*pointing*) Here – it's the temple of Aesculapius.	
Palinurus	(*impatiently*) I've known that for some time.	
Phaedromus	Next to it (*points to the house of Cappadox*) is the dearest door in all the world! (*To door*) Hullo, old friend, I hope I find you well!	
Palinurus	(*mocking*) O *drearest* door in all the world – no touch of fever yesterday, I hope – or the day before that? Have a good dinner yesterday?	
Phaedromus	(*angrily*) Are you making fun of me?	
Palinurus	Well, you must be mad! How can you ask the door if it's *well*?	
Phaedromus	Ah, but this is the sweetest, the discreetest door in existence – it never utters a single word! When it opens – not a sound; when *she* creeps out to see me at night – not a sound then, either!	
Palinurus	You're not … letting yourself or your family down, Phaedromus, sir? You're not going to do that, are you? I trust you're not planning to seduce some decent girl – or some girl who ought to be decent, should I say?	40
Phaedromus	Lord, no! Heaven forbid!	
Palinurus	Heaven forbid indeed. If you're wise, sir, you'll always take care your love affairs are … respectable; then, if rumours get about, your reputation's none the worse for it. Always make sure you can stand up and be counted as a man!	
Phaedromus	Eh? What do you mean by that?	
Palinurus	Watch your step in these love affairs – or you can lose more than you bargained for! *Hm!*	
Phaedromus	But this place is run by a pimp!	
Palinurus	Oh well, in that case, if it's up for sale, no one's	

stopping you from buying, if you've got the money. There's nothing to stop you walking along a public highway – provided you don't trespass on private property, of course – 'wives, widows, virgins, young lads under age and freeborn children of both sexes'! Apart from that, feel free!

Phaedromus This is a pimp's house, I tell you...

Palinurus Well – bad luck to it!

Phaedromus ...and he... 60

Palinurus Serving such a perverted purpose!

Phaedromus (*ironically*) That's it: interrupt me!

Palinurus (*deliberately misunderstanding*) Of course, yes, I will!

Phaedromus Keep quiet.

Palinurus You just told me to interrupt you!

Phaedromus Well, now I'm telling you not to. As I was about to say – he has this young girl –

Palinurus You mean the pimp, the one who lives in this house?

Phaedromus (*impatiently*) That's right. You've got it now!

Palinurus (*smirking*) Good; less risk of losing it!

Phaedromus Oh, don't be so *tiresome*! (*Resuming*) Now he wants to make a whore of her. She's madly in love with me, you see, but I don't want her on loan!

Palinurus Why not?

Phaedromus Because I want her all to myself, that's why! I love her just as much as she loves me.

Palinurus These secret love affairs are bad news – utter ruin, in fact.

Phaedromus You're so right. Lord, you're right! 80

Palinurus Has she been ... er ... broken in yet?

Phaedromus No! I've treated her like my own sister – except for a few kisses, nothing more.

Palinurus Ah, never forget: there's no smoke without fire. Smoke can't burn anything, but flames can! If a man wants to get the kernel from a nut, first he cracks the shell. If a man wants to get a girl into bed, he paves his way with kisses.

Phaedromus But she's a virgin! She's never been with a man, I tell you.

Palinurus If I'd ever heard of a pimp with an ounce of

decency, I could believe that.

Phaedromus Listen! What do you take me for? Whenever she gets a chance to steal out to see me, all she gives me is a quick kiss and then she runs off again. That's because of the pimp, I suppose – he's ill, at the moment, and lying in the temple of Aesculapius[1] here. He's the one who's got it in for me.

Palinurus Why? What's he doing? 99

Phaedromus One moment he asks me for thirty minas for her, the next twice as much! It's no good, I can't get any straight dealing from him at all!

Palinurus You're a fool to expect it: he's a pimp – it's not in him!

Phaedromus What I've done is to send my parasite off to Caria to ask a friend of mine to lend me the money. But if he doesn't bring that back with him, I really don't know where to turn!

Palinurus (*jokingly*) Well, if you're thinking of praying, you turn right, I believe!

Phaedromus You see Venus's altar there in front of their house? That's where I promised to present myself for breakfast.

Palinurus (*deliberately misunderstanding*) Eh? You're going to offer yourself to Venus – for breakfast?

Phaedromus Yes, yes, myself, you, and all these slaves here.

Palinurus You really mean to give the goddess indigestion, don't you!

Phaedromus (*to a slave*) Give the wine-bowl here, boy. 119

Phaedromus moves towards Cappadox's door, the slave following with the wine.

Palinurus What are you up to?

Phaedromus You'll see. There's an old girl who sleeps here, minding the door. Her name's Leaena – a real old dragon, she drinks bucketsful, and she drinks it neat!

Palinurus Dragon? Sounds more like a *flagon* to me – the big sort they keep Chian wine in!

Phaedromus Well, you know what I mean – she's a real drunk! And as soon as I sprinkle some wine over the door

81

here, she knows straight away from the scent that
I'm here, and she opens up at once!

Palinurus And you've brought this bowl of wine for her?

Phaedromus Yes. (*Ironically*) But only if you agree, of course.

Palinurus Well, I don't agree, dammit. And I hope the boy
who's got it falls flat on his face. I thought it was for
us!

Phaedromus Oh, keep quiet, won't you? If she leaves any,
there'll be more than enough for us.

Palinurus *Leave* any? Do you know a river the sea can't
swallow?

Phaedromus This way, Palinurus, come on. (*Takes the bowl*) Do
as I say. 141

Palinurus All right.

Phaedromus (*pouring wine on door sill*) Come, drink, O door of my
delight, drink deep! And prove propitious unto me,
I pray!

Palinurus (*to door, mimicking*) Fancy a few olives, perhaps,
some mincemeat, or a pickled caper?

Phaedromus (*still praying earnestly*) Come, rouse your guardian,
and bring her here to me!

Palinurus (*grabbing Phaedromus*) Here! You're wasting the
wine! What do you think you're doing?

Phaedromus Let go. Look – see the door opening, bless its little
heart? Not so much as a creak, either! That really is
a gem of a hinge!

Palinurus Why don't you give it a kiss then? Go on!

Phaedromus Shh! Let's hide this light and keep quiet!

Palinurus (*bored*) Oh, all right, then.

Leaena comes slowly out of the door, sniffing with interest.

Leaena Aaaah! The fragrance of a rich old wine
Has reached my nostrils – how divine!
Through the dark my desire   160
Draws me onward – I'm on fire!
(*Sniffs*)
Wherever it is, it's somewhere near.
(*With nose close to the door sill*)
Ah bliss! I've found it! Ah, it's *here*!
There you are, darling wine,

82

Bliss of Bacchus, bliss of mine!
You're old, I'm old – come to mother!
We were made for one another!

(*Sniffing with great satisfaction*) Yes, compared with yours, all other perfumes are bilge-water! You are my myrrh, my cinnamon, my rose-water, my essence of violets and lavender; you are the choicest, costliest fragrance I know! Yes, I'd like there to be lots of wine-pouring when they dig my grave!

But a lovely smell's all very well.
My thirst is dire – my throat's on fire.
My nostrils may be satisfied,
But how about my poor inside?   177

(*Sniffing again*) No, it's not the *scent* I want! Where's the wine-bowl itself, that's what I want to know! It's you I'm after, bowl dear, to feel your touch, to pour your lovely liquor into me, and swallow it in gorgeous great gulps! (*Sniffs in Phaedromus's direction*) Aha, it went *this* way! And so shall I!

Phaedromus	(*aside*) The old girl really has a thirst!
Palinurus	How much do you think she could take?
Phaedromus	Oh, nothing out of the way – a few gallons, perhaps.
Palinurus	Good God, from what you say, she could polish off the whole of this year's vintage single-handed!
Phaedromus	With a nose as sensitive as that she ought to have been a hunting dog!
Leaena	Did I hear a voice some way away? Who is it, eh?
Phaedromus	(*aside*) I'd better go and speak to the old girl. Here goes. (*He goes*) Over here, Leaena! Behind you!
Leaena	Who says so?
Phaedromus	Who? Bacchus the maker of mirth, the omnipotent Lord of the Vine, who brings you lubrication when you're hoarse, half asleep, half dead with thirst!
Leaena	(*looking about her*) How far away is He? 200
Phaedromus	See this light? (*Waving his torch*)
Leaena	This way, quickly, then! Don't hang about!

83

Phaedromus	(*going up to her*) Good morning!
Leaena	Good? How can it be good? I'm dying of thirst!
Phaedromus	Well, you'll be drinking soon.
Leaena	(*smacking her lips*) It can't be *too* soon, I tell you.
Phaedromus	(*giving her the bowl*) There you are, dear lady!
Leaena	Ah, bless you, you darling man!
Palinurus	Go on, off you go – swill it all down into the bottomless pit! Flush out your waterworks!
Phaedromus	Quiet! Keep a civil tongue in your head!
Palinurus	(*aside*) I'd rather put a civil fist in hers!
Leaena	(*turning to the altar of Venus*) Venus, accept this tiny offering ... in fact I grudge you every drop! I've not got much, and you're getting even less! After all, you're always getting wine from lovers when they're drinking and want to win your favour. But me – well, gifts like this don't often come my way! (*Drinks the wine greedily*)
Palinurus	Look how she's gulping it all down, the greedy slut! Neat, too, and it's hardly touching the sides! 220
Phaedromus	(*after a pause*) Oh dear, I'm in a fix! Now it comes to it I don't know what to say to her!
Palinurus	Tell her what you just told me.
Phaedromus	What's that?
Palinurus	Tell her you're in a fix.
Phaedromus	Oh, go to blazes!
Palinurus	You tell her that!
Leaena	(*belching*) A-a-r-rgh!
Palinurus	Well? How was that? Nice?
Leaena	(*already feeling the effects*) Nice, yes.
Palinurus	And I think it'd be nice to poke you with the sharp end of a –
Phaedromus	Quiet! (*Threatens him*) Don't you –
Palinurus	No, no, I'll keep quiet! Look! Just look! She's bent over that bowl just like a rainbow![2] There'll be rain later, mark my words!
Phaedromus	Shall I tell her now?
Palinurus	What are you going to say?
Phaedromus	That ... I'm in a fix!
Palinurus	Go on then, tell her that. 240
Phaedromus	(*to Leaena*) Listen, grandmother, there's something

I want to tell you: I'm in a real fix!

Leaena Oh, I'm on top of the world myself!... What's the matter, then? What do you mean, you're in 'a fix'?

Phaedromus Because (*breaking down*) I can't be with the one I love!

Leaena Now don't be upset, Phaedromus dear! You make sure I don't get thirsty, and I'll bring your sweetheart out here in a moment.

Leaena goes into the house.

Phaedromus (*calling after her*) You keep your word, and I'll set up a statue, all of vines instead of gold, as a monument to your outstanding ... thirst! (*Turning*) Palinurus, if she does come out, shan't I be the luckiest man on earth?

Palinurus Ye Gods – a man in love and out of money is in a pretty bad way!

Phaedromus Well, you're wrong – I'm certain that parasite of mine is going to turn up today with the money.

Palinurus That really is optimism – expecting the impossible!

Phaedromus Shall I stand at the door and serenade her? 260

Palinurus If you want to, sir, you go ahead: no good me telling you one way or another – your character's quite changed these days.

Phaedromus Bolts, dear bolts, with joy I greet you,
I beseech you, I entreat you,
Of your magnanimity,
Hear a wretched lover's plea!
Sweetest bolts, be good to me!

Leap like Tuscan tumblers for me!
Jump, I beg you, jump on high!
Send my love out here to cheer me,
Her for whom I pine and die!

Damn those bolts, accursed things!
Have they budged an inch for me?
Not an inch, despite my pleading,
Not an ounce of sympathy!

(*Sulkily*) I see you don't give a *damn* what I feel!...
But wait! Sh! Shh!

Palinurus	I *am* shushing, dammit!
Phaedromus	I can hear something. Oh heavens! I think those bolts are answering my prayer at last! 281

The door opens gradually.

Leaena	(*inside*) Out you come, Planesium dear; quietly now – don't let the door make a noise, or the hinges creak: the master mustn't find out what we're up to! Wait – I'll pour a little water on the hinges here.
Palinurus	(*aside*) Look at the crafty old harridan playing doctor! The medicine *she* takes is neat wine – but when it comes to the door, all she prescribes is water!

Planesium emerges in the doorway. She speaks softly.

Planesium	Where are you? Where is the man who calls me to the Courts of Love? Here I am – answering your call! Now it's your turn to answer mine – come on, show yourself!
Phaedromus	(*in raptures*) Here I am, sweetheart! Imagine me not turning up! Well, if I didn't I'd deserve everything I got!
Planesium	Darling! Please, if you love me, don't stand so far away!
Phaedromus	(*aside to his slave*) Palinurus! Palinurus!
Palinurus	Yes? Why are you calling my name? 300
Phaedromus	She really is *delightful*!
Palinurus	(*cynically*) *Too* delightful, I reckon.
Phaedromus	Oh, I feel like a god!
Palinurus	Wrong again – you're a man – a pretty poor specimen, too.
Phaedromus	What have you ever seen – what'll you ever see more godlike than me?
Palinurus	You're in a pretty bad way, sir; I see that much, and it's got me worried.
Phaedromus	Oh, if you can't be civil, keep quiet!
Palinurus	(*changing tack*) If a man sees his sweetheart and doesn't take his chance with her while he can – well, he only has himself to blame!

Phaedromus   (*to Planesium*) He's quite right – and there's nothing on earth I want more. I've been *longing* for this moment!

Planesium   Hold me, then! Hold me tight!

Phaedromus   (*embracing her*) Ah! This is my only reason for living! Your master may keep us apart, but still I must have you – behind his back!   320

Planesium   Keep us apart? He can't do such a thing! He shan't! Nothing but death will ever come between us!

Palinurus   (*aside*) It's no good, I really can't keep quiet any longer. I must give my master a talking to. It's all right to have a sensible sort of love affair, I suppose – but it's all *wrong* to have the madcap sort! But to go completely *insane* about it – well, that's what my master's doing!

Phaedromus   (*in raptures*) Kings can keep their kingdoms, rich men their riches – they can have their honours, their glorious exploits, their battle glories – let them all keep what belongs to them – so long as they don't envy me my happiness!

Palinurus   Sir? Was it an all-night vigil you promised Venus? Damn me, it'll be daylight soon!

Phaedromus   Quiet, you.

Palinurus   Me keep quiet? Why don't you go home and get some rest, eh?

Phaedromus   I am resting. Shh! *Do not disturb.*

Palinurus   But you're wide awake!   340

Phaedromus   No, this is the way I rest. (*Embracing Planesium and closing his eyes*) This is rest enough for me!

Palinurus   (*to Planesium*) Hey, miss, excuse me! It's not right to do this to my master; he's done nothing to hurt you!

Planesium   (*holding Phaedromus tighter*) You'd be the first to object if you were starving, and he stopped you eating!

Palinurus   (*aside, in disgust*) It's no use, I can see they're both quite hopelessly in love, both insane! Look how madly they're hugging each other, poor fools! They can't get enough of each other. (*To them*) Hey! Break it up, will you?

Planesium   (*sighing*) No human happiness lasts for ever, I

CURCULIO

suppose. It seems ours is to be blighted by this misery here!

Palinurus What's that, you little tart? How *dare* you call me that! You with those owl-eyes of yours – you ... creature of the night, you! You frightful little floosy! You nonentity, you numbskull! 359

Phaedromus Insult her, my *goddess*, would you? You, a mere slave, fit only for flogging, bandying words with his master? You'll regret having said that, by God! You'll be sorry, all right! (*Hits him*) You take that for your foul mouth and learn to think before you speak!

Palinurus (*to Planesium*) Help, help, Venus of ... er ... night vigils!

Phaedromus (*menacingly*) You *won't* keep quiet, will you, you wretch. (*Hits him again*)

Planesium Don't, darling! It's like beating against stone – you'll just hurt your hand!

Palinurus What you're doing, Phaedromus, sir, is perfectly shameful, it's an outrage – laying about someone who's offering you good advice and making love to *this* rubbish! It can't be right for you to lose control of yourself like this!

Phaedromus Find me a lover that can control himself and I'll give you his weight in gold!

Palinurus Find me a master with sense and I'll give you *double* his weight in gold! 380

Planesium I must go, my sweetheart – I can hear the door-bolts rattling; it must be the custodian opening up the temple. But tell me – how long must we go on meeting like this? Must our love *always* be secret?

Phaedromus Not at all! Three days ago I sent my parasite to Caria to get some money. He'll be back today.

Planesium It's all taking so long!

Phaedromus I promise you faithfully – I won't let you spend another three days in that house. Before three days are out you'll be free, as you deserve.

Planesium Well, mind you keep to that. Here – before I go, just one more kiss. (*They kiss*)

Phaedromus Lord! Who would exchange this for a king's

CURCULIO

	ransom? When shall I see you again?
Planesium	For that you'll have to get me freed! If you love me, buy my freedom! Don't keep on asking me the same question over and over again! Pay my purchase price, and I'm yours! Goodbye, my love!

Planesium and Leaena go into the house.

Phaedromus	(*miserably*) Alone again, so soon? Ah, Palinurus, I'm good and done for!
Palinurus	Me too! I'm tired to death, and I nearly got beaten to death!
Phaedromus	(*turning*) Come on.

Phaedromus and Palinurus go into Phaedromus's house. It is now near daybreak. Cappadox, the pimp emerges from the temple of Aesculapius. He is in some discomfort.

Cappadox That's that, then: I'm getting out of the temple right away! It's clear enough Aesculapius doesn't give a damn for me and doesn't want me cured! I get weaker and weaker, and my pain goes from strength to strength. God, when I walk my guts are knotted round me like a belt – it feels as if I'm about to give birth to twins. Ugh! Any moment I may ... burst apart in the middle!

Palinurus enters from the house of Phaedromus.

Palinurus	(*to Phaedromus inside the house*) Take my advice, Phaedromus, and shake off this depression of yours. You're anxious because your parasite hasn't come back from Caria, I know; but I'm sure he's bringing the money – if he weren't, he'd have been back here by now to feed at his usual trough! Wild horses wouldn't have kept him away!
Cappadox	(*looking about*) Who's that?
Palinurus	Who's that I can hear?
Cappadox	Isn't it Palinurus, Phaedromus's man?
Palinurus	(*aside*) Who's that fellow with the corporation and that grassy green look about the eyes? The figure's familiar, but the colouring's ... unusual! Ah, now

I recognise him. It's the pimp Cappadox. I'll have a word with him.

Cappadox Morning, Palinurus.

Palinurus And morning to you, you old rascal! How are you?

Cappadox Oh, surviving – just.

Palinurus (*seeing he is unwell*) No more than you deserve, I reckon! What's the matter, though?

Cappadox My spleen's killing me ... my kidneys ache ... my lungs are ... shattered, my liver's sheer torture ... my heart's riddled and rotting – in fact, all my guts are absolute agony!

Palinurus (*assuming a professional air*) Aha! What you've got is some hepatitic infection, then.

Cappadox Oh, it's easy to laugh at the afflicted. 438

Palinurus Well, just hang on for a few more days, till your insides go completely rotten – it's a good time for pickling, around now. You do that and you'll be able to sell your guts for more than all the rest of you put together!

Cappadox My spleen's ... had it.

Palinurus Well, try walking ... that's best for spleen troubles.

Cappadox Look, be serious for a moment – tell me this: if I told you a dream I had last night, could you interpret it for me?

Palinurus *Could* I? Hah! I happen to be the greatest living authority on divination. Interpreters of dreams come to me to ask my advice! And they treat my answers as holy writ!

A Cook enters from the house of Phaedromus.

Cook What are you standing about for, Palinurus? Why aren't you bringing out the stuff I need? I want the parasite's meal to be ready as soon as he arrives.

Palinurus Wait a moment. I'm interpreting a dream for this chap here.

Cook What? If *you*'ve ever had a dream you always come to *me*! 460

Palinurus (*abashed*) It's true.

Cook Off you go, then. Bring the stuff out.

CURCULIO

Palinurus	(*to Cappadox*) While I see to that, you just tell your dream to him, then. I'll leave you in his hands. He's better at it than I am – he taught me all I know.
Cappadox	I only hope he can help.
Palinurus	He will. (*Goes inside*)
Cappadox	He's a rare sort of servant, that one – actually does what his master tells him! (*To Cook*) Now, are you going to listen?
Cook	Yes. I don't know you at all – but all right.
Cappadox	Last night I dreamed I saw Aesculapius sitting some way away from me, and he didn't make any move to come nearer – in fact, he didn't seem to care two hoots for me!
Cook	Then all the other gods will do the same – you see, they work jointly together on a sort of union basis. It's no wonder you're getting no better – you really ought to have slept in Jupiter's temple – he's the one who's turned a blind eye to all those oaths you've sworn!
Cappadox	If everyone who'd broken an oath decided to spend the night there there wouldn't be enough room on the whole Capitol!
Cook	Listen carefully: you go and beg Aesculapius's pardon, or else you'll find yourself in terrible trouble – the trouble your dream warned you of, in fact.
Cappadox	Thank you, yes; I'll go and say a prayer.

Cappadox goes off into the temple.

Cook	And much bad may it do you!

Cook goes off into Phaedromus's house. Palinurus re-enters from the house.

Palinurus	(*looking into the distance*) Ye Gods – what's this I see? It can't be! No – yes! Isn't it the parasite who was sent off to Caria? Hey – Phaedromus! Come out here! Come out here, I tell you, here, quick!

Phaedromus enters from the house.

91

Phaedromus	What's all the noise about?
Palinurus	I can see your parasite – look, there he is running along, down at the end of the street. He's saying something – let's listen in, shall we?
Phaedromus	(*excited*) Yes, yes, let's! 500

Curculio enters at great speed. He has a patch over one eye.

Curculio Out of my way, all of you, whether I know you or not! I've got a job of work to do! Make way, everyone, I say, off you go, clear the street! I don't want to knock into anyone with my head or my elbow or my chest or knee and do them a mischief! This business of mine is really pressing, I can tell you, urgent, top priority – no one's important enough to stand in my way, I don't care who he is – a general, a dictator even, a market-inspector, chief magistrate or local magistrate – none of them is so grand he can't be knocked flat on his face and go topsy-turvy from the pavement into the street!

Yes, and those Greeks that stride about the city, heads hooded, trailing their cloaks, stalking around, stuffed like a sausage with books and baskets, stopping in groups, gossiping in groups, a race of runabouts; they get in your way, they block your path, they mince about airing their clever ideas – you can always see them knocking it back at the taverns, if they've managed to pinch some money, that is; they swill it down, hot as you like, with their little heads still muffled up, and then they stagger away maudlin and half cut! If I bump into any of *them*, I'll fetch a vegetarian fart out of each and every one of them! 525

Yes, and then those slaves of our young men-about-town who play catch in the street – I'll trample on the lot, throwers and catchers, I'll tread 'em into the ground. If they want to stay clear of trouble, they'd better stay at home!

Phaedromus (*aside*) Sound enough advice, if only there were some way of enforcing it! But that's the way things are with our slaves these days – there's just no way

CURCULIO

	of controlling them.
Curculio	Could anyone tell me where my patron Phaedromus is? I need to see him straight away on urgent business.
Palinurus	(*to Phaedromus*) He's looking for *you*.
Phaedromus	Well, let's go up and say hullo, then. (*Does so*) Hullo! Curculio – I want you. 540
Curculio	Who's that? Who's calling my name?
Phaedromus	Someone who wants to meet you.
Curculio	(*seeing Phaedromus*) No more than I want to meet you, sir!
Phaedromus	Ah, Curculio, bless you, how I've prayed for your return! How good to see you!
Curculio	And you, sir!
Phaedromus	I'm so glad you're safe and sound! Give me your hand, man! Now tell me, for heaven's sake: is my luck in or out?
Curculio	You tell me, for *my* sake: what about *mine*?
Phaedromus	What's the matter?
Curculio	(*tragically*) Ah, my eyes grow dim, my knees are giving way – through lack of nourishment!
Phaedromus	You're tired, that's all.
Curculio	Hold me up, hold me up, for pity's sake!
Phaedromus	Look how pale he's gone! (*Supports Curculio and shouts to slave inside*) Give him a chair to sit on, quickly, and a bowl of water! Hurry up, come on!
Curculio	I'm blacking out! 560
Palinurus	Want some water?
Curculio	So long as it's got something *solid* with it; yes, give it here; let me gulp it down!
Palinurus	You're disgusting!
Curculio	For goodness' sake, now I've *got* here, give me ... something to cool me down!
Palinurus	(*helping Phaedromus to fan him*) Of course.
Curculio	What on earth are you doing?
Palinurus	Cooling you!
Curculio	*That*'s not the sort of draught I need.
Palinurus	What *do* you want, then?
Curculio	A meal! Something to welcome me home!
Palinurus	Oh, to *blazes* with you!

93

Curculio Look, I'm finished – I can hardly see, my teeth are ... all gummed up, my throat's ... er ... streaming with starvation... That's the state I'm in: my guts are gurgling for lack of vital victuals!

Phaedromus You'll have something to eat directly.

Curculio 'Something'? What good's 'something' to me? Couldn't you be *explicit*, sir?   580

Phaedromus Ah, if only you knew the food we've put aside for you!

Curculio It's *where* it is I want to know! God, but my teeth are itching for an introduction!

Phaedromus There's ham, tripe, sow's udders, sausage meat, sweetbreads –

Curculio (*keenly*) Eh? All that? (*Dubiously*) Where? Still locked away in the larder, I suppose.

Phaedromus No, no, already on the plates waiting for you! We knew you'd be arriving any time.

Curculio Look, you're not playing me along, are you?

Phaedromus I'm telling the truth – as I live and love! But you still haven't told me about the errand I sent you on.

Curculio I've got ... nothing.

Phaedromus Then I'm ruined – utterly!

Curculio Well, co-operate with me, sir, and I can *un*ruin you! After I left you, I got to Caria, saw your mate and asked him to lend you the money. Well, he *wanted* to help you – that was obvious – didn't like to disappoint you – after all, friends are there to help each other out, he said. He didn't have much to say, but he was quite frank about it. He said you and he were in exactly the same boat – *both* short of funds!

Phaedromus Every word you speak is a mortal blow!   604

Curculio On the contrary, I can save you, and that's just what I aim to do. When he told me this, I went off to the market place. I was really annoyed at having gone on such a wild goose chase. Just by chance, I saw a military type there – well, up I went and said hullo to him. 'Hullo,' says he, and grabbed my hand, took me on one side and asked me what had brought me to Caria. 'Oh, just a pleasure trip,' I told him. Then he asks me if I knew a banker in

Epidaurus called Lyco. I said I did. 'What about a
pimp named Cappadox?' I said yes, I'd often gone
to his establishment. 'What about him?' I asked.
'Well,' he says, 'I bought a girl off him for thirty
minas, and her clothing and jewellery as well – that
was an extra ten.' 'You gave him the money, did
you?' I said. 'No,' he says, 'it's all deposited with
that banker Lyco I mentioned. I've told him
someone will bring him a letter from me sealed with
my signet ring, and he's to help him to get the girl
from the pimp – *plus* the jewellery and clothes.'
After he'd told me all this, I went off, but he called
me back straight away and invited me to dinner.
Well, I couldn't refuse – it's against my principles,
anyway! 'Why don't we go home and relax?' he
said. It seemed a good idea to me. 'Why waste
time?' I agreed. 'Never put off till tomorrow what
you can eat today!' 'Everything's ready!' he says.
Well, ready it was, and we were ready for it, too,
when we got there! After we'd had dinner and
drunk plenty of wine, he called for dice and chal-
lenged me to a game. I put down my cloak as a
stake, and he bet his ring against it; then, as he
made his throw he called out the name – *Planesium*!

Phaedromus	(*starts*) My sweetheart? *Planesium*?	638
Curculio	Listen a moment!... He threw four Ones. I grabbed the dice, called on my fairy godmother Greedyguts, and threw a Royal Flush! I filled an enormous cup and drank his health: he drained it off to the last drop, his head dropped and he went out like a light! I slipped off his ring and got off the couch as quietly as I could, so he shouldn't hear. The servants asked me where I was off to, and I said I was going where men do go when they've had a skinful. Soon as I saw the front door I made a dash for it!	
Phaedromus	Oh, well *done*!	
Curculio	Save that until I've actually pulled this off! Let's go indoors now and make up that letter!	
Phaedromus	Yes, let's; straight away!	

Curculio   And *first* of all let's force down something solid –
some ham, sow's udder, sweetbreads – that'll line
the stomach well enough – and some bread and
roast beef, with a king-sized cup to go with it –
bucketloads of wine, in fact – we mustn't run out of
... er, ideas! You can write the letter, Palinurus
here can be our waiter. I'll – I'll concentrate on the
eating! I'll tell you how to write it. Come on – in you
come! (*Makes eagerly for the door*)   662

Phaedromus   (*excitedly*) I'm right behind you!

*Curculio, Phaedromus and Palinurus go inside. The banker
Lyco enters.*

Lyco   I seem to be in luck! I've been doing my sums to
calculate my debits and credits, and I'm a rich man
– so long as I don't pay my creditors! (If I do pay
them, though, my liabilities outweigh my assets!)
Really, though, to be serious about it, if they press
me too hard, I'll have to go bankrupt. That's the
way with most bankers – they go round chasing
everyone else to pay their debts, but never pay their
own – and if anyone makes a fuss about it, they
settle accounts with their fists! If anyone makes
money quickly, he'd better be quick to economise,
too, or just as quickly he's on the breadline! What
I'd really like to do is to buy a young lad and hire
him out to bring in some cash – God, how I *need
money*!   678

*Curculio and a slave appear in the doorway of Phae-
dromus's house.*

Curculio   (*to Phaedromus inside*) I've got it, I know – no need to
keep reminding me now I'm full! Leave it to me –
I'll succeed, all right. Don't you worry! (*Stepping
forward*) Whew! I really did *stuff* myself in there –
but I still left one little corner of my stomach free
for lining with what's left of the leftovers! (*Sees Lyco*)
Who's this fellow with his head all muffled, paying
his respects to Aesculapius? Aha! The very man I
was looking for! (*To the slave*) Follow me – I'm going

96

to pretend I don't know him. (*Aloud*) Hey, I'd like a word with you!

Lyco Morning, One-eye!

Curculio (*indignant*) Are you making fun of me?

Lyco You must be one of that Cyclops tribe, I reckon – they're a one-eyed lot.

Curculio This eye was knocked out by a catapult at Sicyon, I'll have you know!

Lyco Look – it could have been knocked out by a broken pot full of cinders for all I care!

Curculio (*aside*) Blimey! He must be clairvoyant, this one! That's *exactly* what happened! I often get fired at by artillery of that sort! (*Aloud*) Young fellow, I got this – er, underneath here doing my bit for the country, it's an honourable scar, and I'll thank you not to poke fun at me in public. 703

Lyco How about letting me poke it for fun in *private*, then, eh?

Curculio You'll do nothing like that with *me*, I can tell you! I don't want any sort of meeting like that with *your* sort, public or private! But I'd be grateful to you – really and truly grateful, if you could tell me where I can find someone – I'm looking for Lyco the banker.

Lyco (*cautiously*) Tell me why you're after him. Where have you come from?

Curculio All right – I'm on an errand for Captain Therapontigonus Platagidorus.

Lyco (*aside*) Lord – I know *that* name all right! How could I forget it? I filled four whole pages when I wrote it down in my ledger! (*Aloud*) Why are you looking for Lyco?

Curculio I was asked to deliver this letter (*shows it*) to him.

Lyco Who are you? 721

Curculio His freedman – they call me Enureticus.

Lyco Enureticus, eh? Pleased to meet you. But why *Enureticus*?

Curculio Well, when I go to bed drunk, er . . . somehow my clothes get wet. *That*'s why!

Lyco You'd better look elsewhere for a bed, then – I've

no room for a wet-blanket like you at my place, I can tell you! However ... I'm the man you're looking for.

Curculio You are? Really? Lyco the banker?

Lyco That's me, yes.

Curculio Therapontigonus told me to give you his warmest best wishes, and this letter.

Lyco Me?

Curculio Yes. There you are – look at the seal.

Lyco Of course; an armed warrior slicing an elephant in two with his sword.

Curculio He told me to say he'll be much obliged if you act for him without delay.   740

Lyco Stand aside one moment – I'll take a look at what he's written.

Curculio Of course, anything, so long as you give me what I came for.

Lyco (*reading*) 'Capt. Therapontigonus Platagidorus sends cordial greetings to his friend Lyco at Epidaurus.'

Curculio (*aside*) He's swallowing it – hook, line and sinker!

Lyco ... 'Be so kind as to hand over to the bearer of this letter the girl I purchased over there, together with her jewellery and clothes – as formally agreed, in your presence and by your agency. You know what we arranged: you are to give the money to the pimp, and the girl to my representative.' (*To Curculio*) Well, where is the Captain? Why hasn't he come himself?

Curculio I'll tell you why: we only arrived in Caria three days ago from India. He wants to have a statue of himself made there, of solid gold, seven foot high, to commemorate all his exploits.

Lyco What for?   760

Curculio I'll tell you: because, inside twenty days, single handed, he conquered the Persians Paphlagonians Sinopians Arabs Carians Cretans Syrians Rhodians Lycians Gluttonians Dipsomanians, er ... the Centauromachians, the army of the Singletittians, all the country of Libya, and the whole of Grapetreadonia! (*Takes a deep breath*) In fact, about

	half the people of the entire world!
Lyco	Whew!
Curculio	Surprised?
Lyco	Shut all that lot up in a coop like chickens and you couldn't walk round them in a whole twelvemonth! ... Yes, I can believe you're his man all right – you talk such blathering *nonsense*!
Curculio	I'll tell you more, if you like!
Lyco	No *thanks*! (*Moves off*) Come with me, and I'll settle this business of yours.

Cappadox the pimp enters from the temple.

	Aha! here he is! Good morning to you, pimp!
Cappadox	(*unenthusiastically*) The same to you.
Lyco	I've some business to do with you.
Cappadox	Well? What is it?
Lyco	Here's your money – take it, and let this fellow here take the girl.
Cappadox	What about the oath I swore?
Lyco	What does it matter so long as you get your money?
Cappadox	Ah well, 'Good advice is beyond price,' they say! This way, gentlemen.

Cappadox goes towards his house.

Curculio	No time-wasting now, pimp!

Lyco, Cappadox and Curculio go into the house. Enter the Choragus, or Stage Property Manager.

Choragus	(*eyeing the retreating Curculio*) Well, well, well – Phaedromus has got himself a plausible rogue and no mistake! I don't know which description's more accurate – twister or shyster! I wonder if I'll ever get back the costume I lent him! Although it wasn't him I dealt with – it was Phaedromus. Still, I'm going to keep an eye on him. Well – till he comes out again, my friends, I'll fill in time by telling you where you can find any type of man you want – perverted or virtuous, honest or dishonest – where you can look to save yourselves time and trouble.

If it's a perjurer you want, go straight to the law-

780

799

99

courts! A liar and a braggart? – the temple of Venus
the Purifier! Look for wealthy husbands on the
loose in the Basilica. That's where you'll see
clapped-out old tarts, too, and the men who haggle
over them! Want to make up a bottle party? Look
in the Fishmarket. At the lower end of the Forum
the real gentlemen stroll about, the ones with
money; in the middle, near the Canal, you get the
dandies, who just like to be seen. Above the lake,
the know-all gossips congregate – malicious types
who run down other people mercilessly, and really
ought to hear some home truths about themselves!
Below the Old Colonnade you'll find the money-
lenders, putting out and borrowing money on interest. Then, behind the Temple of Castor are types
you'd be ill advised to trust on a brief acquaint-
ance. In the Tuscan Quarter you get the male prostitutes, who'll turn their hands to anything – or
anyone! In the Velabrum, butchers and bakers and
oracle makers. And for rich husbands on the
rampage, look in the house of Oppian Leucadia!

But listen! The door's opening – I'd better pipe
down.   823

*The Choragus goes off. Curculio comes out of the house, fol-
lowed by a slave, Cappadox, Lyco and Planesium.*

Curculio	You go first, young lady – I can't keep an eye on you if you're behind me. (*To Cappadox*) The Captain said all the jewellery and clothes she had were his, too.
Lyco	No one's denying it.
Curculio	Well, I just thought I'd remind you.
Lyco	(*to Cappadox*) And you remember – if anyone goes to court and establishes that she's freeborn, you promised I get my money back, all thirty minas of it!
Cappadox	I'll remember – don't fuss. What I said still stands.
Curculio	Well, make jolly sure you do remember!
Cappadox	I remember. It'll all be fair and square, I guarantee.

100

Curculio	Fair and square? A guarantee from a pimp? That's new. The only guarantee a pimp's got is a tongue to talk his way out of his debts! The goods you sell and set free and order about aren't yours by rights at all. You've no legal title to them and you can't give the title to anyone else, either. In my view your whole pimping profession has the same social prestige as flies, as gnats, bugs, lice, fleas! You're just a nuisance, a pest, a menace – no damn good to anyone! No decent citizen feels comfortable standing next to you in public – and if anyone does, people run him down, stare at him, abuse him for it – even if he's done nothing at all, people speak about him as if he's a lost cause – a nothing, beneath contempt!

851

Lyco	You know your pimps all right, my one-eyed friend!
Curculio	(*angrily, to Lyco*) Well, I put you bankers in exactly the same category, damme if I don't! You're just like pimps. But at least pimps do their business in private – you do yours in public, in the Forum! You both ruin men: they do it with their filthy soliciting and their dens of iniquity, you do it with your interest rates! It's all your fault the people have to pass so many laws; and no sooner are they passed, than you break them! You always find some loophole or other! No, to you lot, laws stay hot about as long as water!

864

Lyco	(*swallowing*) I should've kept quiet!
Cappadox	Well said! You've every reason to abuse the banking fraternity!
Curculio	Abuse? I call it abuse if it's undeserved; if it's deserved, I reckon it's 'fair comment'. Anyway, I've no time for any guarantee you can offer me, nor for any other pimp's. (*Moves to go*) I'm off. All right?
Lyco	Goodbye.
Curculio	Goodbye. (*Turns away*)
Cappadox	(*to Curculio*) Hey, you – you there!
Curculio	Well? What do you want?
Cappadox	Take care the girl is well looked after ... she was

101

	decently brought up at my place ... not a hand was laid on her.
Curculio	If you're so worried about her, what'll you give me to see she's looked after properly? 880
Cappadox	Oh, drop dead!
Curculio	Why don't *you*? Just the medicine to sort you out!
Cappadox	(*to Planesium*) What are you crying for, you little fool? Don't worry – I got a good price for you – it's a rich place you're going to! Make sure to behave yourself now; be a good girl and go along with him without a fuss.
Lyco	Well, Enureticus, that's that, I think.
Curculio	Yes. Goodbye, and good luck. Thank you for your time *and* for the money!
Lyco	Give my regards to your patron.
Curculio	I will.

Curculio leads Planesium off.

Lyco	(*to Cappadox*) Well, I'll be off.
Cappadox	Wait – what about that other ten minas for the jewellery and clothes? I need something to live on while I'm convalescing, you see – for medical expenses. 897
Lyco	You'll get them. Send round for them tomorrow.

Lyco goes off.

Cappadox	Well, that's all completed satisfactorily, so I think I'll just pop into the temple and say a word of thanks! I only paid ten minas for the girl, too – oh, long ago when she was a baby. I never saw the man who sold her to me again; I suppose he must be dead. Still, what do I care? I've got the cash! Yes, if the gods love a man, they always throw money his way! ... Now I'll go and offer thanks – I really *must* look after myself properly.

Cappadox goes into the temple. Therapontigonus and Lyco enter.

Therapont	(*roaring*) Angry? I'm angry, by God, but this isn't any *ordinary* anger! I'm absolutely *fuming*! Just the

way I feel when I smash cities into the dust! If you don't give back those thirty minas I left with you this moment, it'll be the last moment you remember, I promise you that!

Lyco (*imitating*) And I'll teach you a lesson, by God – it won't be any *ordinary* lesson, either – it'll be the sort I usually give people who lie about owing me money!

Therapont Don't try to scare me – and don't think I'm going to plead with you, either! 919

Lyco And don't think you're ever going to make me give back what I've already given back! Because I won't!

Therapont I *thought* you might not give it back when I handed it over to you.

Lyco Well, why are you asking for it back, then?

Therapont I want to know who you gave it to.

Lyco Your freedman, the one-eyed fellow – said his name was Enureticus.

Therapont One-eyed freedman – Enureticus? What on earth are you talking about? I haven't got a freedman – not one!

Lyco You're smarter than pimps are, at least: they set slaves free, and never give them another thought!

Therapont What *have* you done?

Lyco What you told me to do: you said I was to deal with a messenger you would send, who'd be bringing me your seal.

Therapont You must be the biggest fool on earth! Trusting a letter! 939

Lyco Why shouldn't I? All public and private business is done through letters. I'm off now. The account's settled. (*Salutes*) Fare well, then, Agamemnon!

Therapont What do you mean, 'fare *well*'?

Lyco All right, then, wither away and drop dead, for all I care!

Lyco goes off.

Therapont What am I going to do now? A fat lot of good it was making princes crawl and lick my boots, if a lazy layabout like *him* can make a fool of me and get away with it!

Cappadox enters from the temple.

Cappadox   When the gods smile on a man, I don't think they can be too angry with him. Well, I made my offering, then it occurred to me I should go and ask for those extra ten minas owing to me – just in case the banker decided to do a bunk. I don't see why he should get fat at *my* expense!

Therapont   (*truculently*) I said good day to you.

Cappadox   Therapontigonus Platagidorus, hullo! Welcome back to Epidaurus! Come on round to my place – and go without your supper!   959

Therapont   Too kind of you, but I'd already decided – to see you in hell first! Well, what about that ... er, purchase of mine you've got at home?

Cappadox   I've nothing of yours at home; I don't owe you a thing.

Therapontigonus begins to get very excited.

No, there's no need for witnesses!

Therapont   *What?*

Cappadox   I did exactly what I promised to do.

Therapont   Are you going to give me that girl or not, you scum? Or d'you want me to skewer you with this sword of mine?

Cappadox   (*unperturbed*) Oh, go and take a running jump at yourself! Don't you try and scare me! They've come for the girl already, and they'll come to collect you too, I'm telling you, if you keep on insulting me. All you'll collect from me's a black eye!

Therapont   You dare threaten *me* with a black eye?

Cappadox   That's right. And I'll give you one, too, if you go on bothering me!   978

Therapont   A pimp threaten *me*? *Me*? Thumb his nose at my military medals, my brilliant bravery in battle? No! By my sword and buckler, my trusted helpers in time of battle, if I don't get the girl back, I'll take you apart so thoroughly the ants'll be able to carry

104

	you off in tiny pieces!
Cappadox	(*mimicking him*) And by my hair-tweezers, my comb, mirror, curling-tongs, scissors and bath-towel – your big talk and your blustering babble mean as much to me as the slave girl who scrubs out my loo! I gave the girl to your fellow who brought the cash.
Therapont	Who was that?
Cappadox	Said he was your freedman, Enureticus.
Therapont	My – ? (*Suddenly seeing light*) Ah! Now I think it over, I *see*. It's Curculio who's done this to me – he's the one who stole my ring.
Cappadox	Lost your ring, have you? (*Aside*) A fine sort of officer! Just the type for a posting in the No-Pay Corps!
Therapont	Where can I find Curculio now?
Cappadox	Curculio? Why settle for *one* weevil? You'll find millions of them in among the corn! I'm off now. All the best!
Therapont	And all the worst to you, damn you!

998

Cappadox goes off.

What am I going to do? Hang around here, or go? Imagine – *me* being made a fool of, like this! Oh, what wouldn't I give to the man who could show me where Curculio is!

Enter Curculio from the house of Phaedromus.

Curculio	I heard an old dramatist wrote in some tragedy that 'Two women are worse than one.' They are, too – but I never saw or heard of a worse example than Phaedromus's girl! I can't even *imagine* one worse! As soon as she saw this ring (*holds up the ring*) of mine she asked where I'd got it. 'What d'you want to know that for?' I asked. 'Because I've got to know,' she says. I said I wasn't telling her. Then she grabbed hold of me and even bit me to try and tear it off! I only just managed to get away from her and come out here! I'm having no more truck with the little bitch!

Enter Planesium, followed by Phaedromus.

Planesium	Phaedromus, hurry!

105

Phaedromus	Why the hurry? 1020
Planesium	You'll let him get away! Oh, it means so *much* to me!
Curculio	(*ruefully*) Well it can't be me she wants – I've got *nothing*! What little I did have I got through in no time!
Phaedromus	(*grabbing Curculio*) I've got him! What's it all about?
Planesium	Ask him where he got that ring. It's the one my own father used to wear!
Curculio	(*indignantly*) It belonged to my mother's sister!
Planesium	My mother gave it to him.
Curculio	And – don't tell me – your father gave it to you?
Planesium	You're talking rubbish!
Curculio	I do, yes. I find it's easier to make a living that way! Now what's all this about?
Planesium	Please – *please* help – let me find my parents?
Curculio	Eh? Your parents? *Me?* (*Looks hard at the ring*) Think I've got them hidden away under the stone here, do you?
Planesium	I was born *free*, I tell you!
Curculio	So were lots of other slaves! 1040
Phaedromus	(*to Curculio*) Look, I'm beginning to lose my temper!
Curculio	But I told you how I got hold of this – how many times have I got to tell you? I tricked a soldier at a game of dice.

Enter Therapontigonus.

Therapont	(*aside, seeing Curculio*) Thank goodness – the very man I was looking for! (*Aloud*) And how are you, my fine fellow?
Curculio	All ears, all ears... How would you fancy the best of three throws – for that cloak of yours? Fancy dicing?
Therapont	To hell with you – you and your dicing and onion-slicing! Give me back my money or the girl!
Curculio	What money? What are you babbling about? What girl is it you want?
Therapont	The one you got from the pimp today, you twister!
Curculio	But I didn't.

Therapont	Damn me, there she *is*! I can see her with my own eyes!
Phaedromus	(*quietly*) This girl is free. 1059
Therapont	What d'you mean 'free'? My own slave girl? *I* never freed her!
Phaedromus	Who gave you any rights to her? Who did you buy her from? Tell me that.
Therapont	I paid the money for her through my banker. And I'll get it back from you and the pimp – four times over!
Phaedromus	(*angry*) Trade in kidnapped girls, would you – free-born girls? Right – off to court with you!
Therapont	I'm not moving!
Phaedromus	(*to Curculio*) Hear that? Will you witness this for me in court?
Therapont	He can't. He's a slave, he's your *dependant*!
Phaedromus	Damn you – I hope your dependants ... drop off! Both of 'em! (*To Curculio again*) Now, Curculio, I'm asking you formally to be my witness. I have the right. Come here.
Therapont	A slave give evidence in court?

Phaedromus touches Curculio's ear in the formal gesture.[3]

Curculio	See? I'm free. There's proof. You're going to court!
Therapont	Try this for size! (*Hits Curculio*)
Curculio	(*shouting hysterically*) Help, citizens, help! 1080
Therapont	What's all the yelling for?
Phaedromus	What did you hit him for?
Therapont	I felt like it.
Phaedromus	(*to Curculio*) Come here, Curculio. I'm handing this fellow over to you.
	Curculio begins to whimper with fright.
	Oh, be quiet!
Planesium	Phaedromus, oh please, please help me!
Phaedromus	I will, don't worry – as if my own soul depended on it! (*To Therapontigonus*) Captain – would you kindly tell me where you got that ring – the one Curculio here took from you?
Planesium	Yes – (*falling at Therapontigonus's feet*) do tell us please – I'm *begging* you!

107

Therapont	(*coolly*) What's it to you two? Why don't you ask me where I got my cloak and sword, too, while you're about it?
Curculio	Fancies himself, doesn't he!
Therapont	Forget *him* (*nodding at Curculio*). All right, I'll tell you the whole story. 1099
Curculio	(*to Phaedromus*) Rubbish! He can't tell you a thing!
Planesium	Tell me, *please* tell me!
Therapont	I will. (*To Planesium*) Up you get! Now then, listen closely. My father Periphanes wore it –
Planesium	*Periphanes!*
Therapont	– and before he died he gave it to me – his own son, as was right and proper.
Planesium	Good Lord!
Therapont	So he made me his heir.
Planesium	Gods above! If I have been true to my family's memory, help me now! (*Falls on Therapontigonus*) My brother, my own *brother!*
Therapont	Eh? How am I supposed to believe that? All right, if you're telling the truth, who was your mother?
Planesium	Cleobula.
Therapont	And your nurse?
Planesium	Archestrata. She had taken me to see the Festival of Dionysus. But no sooner had we got there than a terrible gale blew up, and the seating gave way and I was petrified. Someone snatched me up – I don't know who – I was so scared, half dead with fright! I can't begin to tell you how it all happened. 1121
Therapont	Yes, I remember there was a disturbance. But tell me now – where's the man who carried you off?
Planesium	I don't know, but I've always kept this ring with me. (*Holds up her hand*) I had it with me the day I disappeared.
Therapont	Give it here! Let me see that!
Curculio	(*to Planesium*) Are you mad? I wouldn't give it to *him!*
Planesium	No – let me be. (*Gives it to Therapontigonus*)
Therapont	Heavens above! This is the one I gave you on your birthday! I know it as well as I know my own face! Sister! My own sister! (*Embracing her*)

108

Planesium	Oh, my dear brother!
Phaedromus	Well, well! Bless you both!
Curculio	God bless us every one, I say! (*To Therapontigonus*) Captain, you should celebrate your arrival today by giving a dinner in your sister's honour! Phaedromus here will give one tomorrow in honour of his bride! (*Waits for an offer*) All right, we accept!
Phaedromus	Keep quiet, you. 1141
Curculio	I won't – seeing everything's turned out so nicely! Captain, sir, how about agreeing to your sister's marriage to Phaedromus here? I'll give her a dowry myself.
Therapont	What sort of dowry are you offering?
Curculio	Me? Oh, er – the right to keep me in food as long as she lives. I mean it, too.
Therapont	(*laughing*) I'll agree to that! (*Changing tone*) And now the pimp owes us thirty minas!
Phaedromus	Why?
Therapont	Because he promised me if anyone established that the girl was freeborn he'd pay me back the lot without any argument. Now – let's find the pimp!
Curculio	A good idea!
Phaedromus	But first I've business to settle.
Therapont	What's that?
Phaedromus	Will you agree to your sister marrying me?
Curculio	Yes, come on, Captain, give your consent.
Therapont	If that's what she wants. 1160
Planesium	Oh yes, I do! More than anything!
Therapont	Very well, so be it.
Curculio	That's the way!
Phaedromus	You agree then, sir? The engagement's formal?
Therapont	Yes.
Curculio	Same here – I agree.
Therapont	Too kind! (*Looks down street*) But look – here's the pimp coming – Mister Money in person!

Cappadox enters in a hurry.

Cappadox	People who say you're a fool to trust bankers are talking nonsense. You can be lucky or unlucky, I say – and I proved it myself today. If you hand over

your money to men that don't pay up, you're not depositing it – you're kissing it goodbye! Take Lyco, for example – he went round all the banks trying to raise the money he owed me. But it was no good, so I kicked up a fuss and demanded my money, and he invited me to sue him. Well, I thought I'd have to go before the praetor to settle matters with him, and that really put the wind up me. But his friends finally won him over and he paid up out of his own capital. And now that's all over I'm going straight home! (*Goes towards his house*)

Therapont	Hey, you, pimp! I want a word with you! 1183
Phaedromus	And so do I.
Cappadox	(*looking back quickly*) But I don't want a word with either of you!
Therapont	Stop right where you are!
Phaedromus	Yes – and cough up that money, come on! Be quick about it!
Cappadox	(*to Therapontigonus*) What do you want with me? (*To Phaedromus*) Or you?
Therapont	Me? I'm going to make a human javelin out of you, and fire you from a siege catapult! God, I'll send you flying, you twister!
Phaedromus	No – a smart young fellow like you deserves *spoiling*! I'm going to give you a pet to cuddle at night – a cat o' nine tails, I mean!
Cappadox	And I'm going to see you both rot in gaol!
Phaedromus	Right! Grab him by the scruff of the neck! Off to the gallows and to hell with him! 1200
Therapont	Hell? He'll be going there anyway! (*He grabs Cappadox*)
Cappadox	For the love of heaven, stop! You can't drag me away like this without a trial or even witnesses! Please, Planesium and Phaedromus, I'm begging you – help me!
Planesium	(*to Therapontigonus*) Please, don't take the law into your own hands like this! He always treated me respectfully at his house, he never laid a finger on me.

Therapont	Hm, not through choice, I reckon – you can thank Aesculapius here (*points to the temple*) that you're still a virgin. If he'd been fit enough to run his business properly he'd have been packing you off to all the clients he could find long ago!
Phaedromus	(*to Therapontigonus and Cappadox*) Listen here, you two: let me see if I can't settle this argument of yours. (*To Therapontigonus*) Let go of him. *Therapontigonus releases Cappadox.* Come here, pimp. If you're both willing to accept my ruling, I'll tell you what I think.
Therapont	All right. We'll let you settle it, then. 1220
Cappadox	Provided you rule no one gets a penny out of me!
Therapont	Eh? What about the money you promised me?
Cappadox	Promised? *How?*
Therapont	Verbally.
Cappadox	Well, I verbally *deny* it. God gave me my tongue for talking with, not beggaring myself with!
Phaedromus	He's wasting time. Get him by the neck!

Therapontigonus advances.

Cappadox	Er, hold on! I'll do as I'm told!
Therapont	Now you're talking sense! Answer me this.
Cappadox	Ask me what you like.
Therapont	Did you, or did you not, promise that if anyone proved this girl was freeborn, you'd give back all the money?
Cappadox	Er – I don't recall saying that.
Therapont	What? Do you *deny* it?
Cappadox	Yes, I do, I deny it. Did anyone witness it? Where were we when I said it?
Therapont	You said it in front of me and the banker Lyco.
Cappadox	Liar!
Therapont	I'm not lying! 1240
Cappadox	I don't give two hoots for you – it's no use trying to scare me!
Therapont	(*to Phaedromus*) He promised in front of me and Lyco.
Phaedromus	I quite believe you. (*To Cappadox*) Now look here, pimp: here's what I've decided. This girl is free,

CURCULIO

and this gentleman's her brother – she's his own sister – got it? – and she's going to be my wife! You give my brother-in-law his money back. *That's* my decision!

Therapont And if I don't get the money back, you're going straight to gaol!

Cappadox Dam*nation*! Phaedromus, that's a bent decision if ever I heard one! You'll be sorry for this – and as for you, Captain, God rot you! (*Turns to go*) Oh, all right, come with me, then.

Therapont Where are we going?

Cappadox To my bankers – to court! That's where I settle all my debts!

Therapont It'll be gaol for you – not the court, if you don't give me back my money!   1261

Cappadox Oh, drop dead, won't you? I really wish you would!

Therapont Oh really?

Cappadox Yes, *really*.

Therapont See these fists of mine? (*Clenches them*)

Cappadox Yes – what about them?

Therapont What about them? Just give me an excuse and I'll shut your mouth with these, double quick!

Cappadox (*frightened suddenly*) Er – all right; come on, then (*taking the money from a purse*), have your money now.

Therapont I will. (*Takes it*) *Thank* you!

Phaedromus Have dinner with me tonight, Captain! The wedding takes place today!

Therapont Good luck to you both – and to all of us! (*Turning to audience*) Friends, your appreciation, please!

NOTES TO CURCULIO

1 It was the custom for sick people to sleep in the temple of Aesculapius in the hope of having inspired dreams which would reveal how they might be cured.
2 The rainbow was thought to be drinking where it touched the earth.

3 Touching the ear was the customary procedure for securing a man's service as a witness. Only a free man could be called on to act in this way.

Casina

Casina, who gives her name to the play, is a slavegirl who was rescued from exposure as a baby (in ancient times this was a common method of getting rid of unwanted babies) and brought up in the household of Lysidamus. Both he, an old man now, and his son have fallen for the girl, and in order to gain access to her, the father has instructed his farm-manager, Olympio, to ask for her hand in marriage, while his son has given the same orders to Chalinus, his orderly (presumably he had served in the army). The old man's wife, Cleostrata, discovers what is going on, and tries her utmost to thwart her husband's philandering. When stalemate is reached, the rival slaves are made to draw lots, and the lottery comes out in Olympio's favour. Lysidamus eagerly arranges a night with the bride at his neighbour's house. But Cleostrata and Chalinus plot a counter-intrigue, in order to frustrate him. First, Casina is said to be out of her mind; then Chalinus himself dresses up as the bride, and finally Lysidamus is betrayed by his own man, Olympio, and is disgraced, as he so richly deserves to be, but finally forgiven.

Casina is a hilarious, swift-moving farce, but, because of its subject-matter, it has been considered by some critics to be offensive, to go too far. But, significantly, this is the one play of Plautus we know to have been revived (lines 7–26 of the Prologue were specially composed after Plautus's death for a revival which is likely to have taken place in the years 165–155 B.C.), and it was extremely popular in antiquity. It is easy to see why; and, as we read the play today, we should remember that the original was in verse, and only part of it was spoken verse. In *Casina* (usually dated in 185 or 184 B.C. because of the reference to the Senate's Decree about the Bacchanalia, lines 1547 ff.) there is an enormous amount of sung lyric verse (see Introduction pp. 3–4). The scenes alternate sung and spoken verse in a very lively way to provide the maximum variety, and this play is therefore thought to be one of Plautus's most mature creations.

It should be noted that neither *Casina* nor the unmarried son of Lysidamus appears, although they are essential characters to the plot. The Prologue and Epilogue inform us that the foundling girl will be discovered as the daughter of Lysidamus's neighbours, a freeborn Athenian girl, and will be married (once she is known to be free and Athenian, she is permitted to marry) to the son of Lysidamus. But the recognition-scene (so common a feature of Greek New Comedy), and the marriage of the lovers, are not parts of Plautus's play, though they may have formed the climax of the original by Diphilus. Also, it seems likely that the suppression of the young man's part, the impersonation of the bride by Chalinus, and the burlesque ending, are Plautus's work. The Greek original was called *Cleroumenoe* ('The Drawers of Lots'). Plautus's Latin version was apparently called the same (*Sortientes*), and probably *Casina* was the title only of the revival.

Towards the end of the play the text is in places quite badly mutilated. Rather than leave gaps, I have invented the sort of thing that might have appeared in the original.

Casina

CHARACTERS

Olympio	Farm bailiff of Lysidamus
Chalinus	Town slave of Lysidamus
Cleostrata	Lysidamus's wife
Pardalisca	Her maid
Myrrhina	Cleostrata's next door neighbour
Lysidamus	Old Athenian gentleman
Alcesimus	Myrrhina's husband, Lysidamus's friend
Citrio	A cook
Cleostrata's maids	
Slaves in Lysidamus's household	
Citrio's assistants	

The scene is set in a street in Athens, outside the houses of Lysidamus and Alcesimus. The speaker of the Prologue enters. He begins formally.

Prologue   (*grandly*) Welcome to all you worthy spectators, who have such a high regard for Honesty – as Honesty has for you! (*Confidentially*) If what I've said is the truth, give me a round of applause so I can be sure right from the start that you'll give me a fair hearing.   6

(*He waits*)

Those of you who drink old wine, and enjoy watching the old plays, are no fools, to my way of thinking. It follows that, since you like the old-time workmanship and writing, you like the old plays better than the rest. These new comedies they're producing nowadays are even poorer quality than the new coins we use! Now, since we found out from local gossip that you're really keen to see the plays

116

of Plautus again, we're presenting an old comedy of
his which those of you who are getting on in years
enjoyed at the time. The younger ones won't know
it, I'm sure; but we'll do our best to put that right!
Now when this play was first put on, it threw all
others in the shade. That was the golden age of
poets, then; they've all gone now, gone the way of
all flesh. Still, even though they can't be here in
person, they can give us just as much pleasure as if
they were. Now I appeal to all of you to give our
company your kind attention. Forget all your cares
and worries about the money you owe – no one
must think about the debt-collector today! The
Games are on, it's a day of rest – it's even a *Bank*
Holiday! Everything's quiet; in the City they're cel-
ebrating the ... Festival of Repose. With the
bankers it's all calculated: when the Games are on,
they won't chase anyone for their money; but afterwards, they won't return yours in a hurry, either!

Now, if you've got a spare ear, pay attention: I
want to give you the title of this comedy. It is called
CLEROUMENOE in Greek, SORTIENTES in Latin. Diphilus wrote it in Greek, and then Plautus wrote a
new version in Latin – Plautus, the comic with the
canine connexions![1]   39

An old gentleman, a married man, lives hereabouts. He has a son who lives in that house there
(*he points to the house of Lysidamus*) with him. He also
has a slave who is lying at death's door – no, no, 'in
bed' I should have said, to be truthful. This slave –
(*breaking off*) but it all happened sixteen years ago
now, when he saw a baby girl being abandoned one
day at the crack of dawn. He went straight up to
the woman who was abandoning the baby and
begged her to give it him; he got her to agree, too,
and took the baby away with him. He carried it
straight home, gave it to his mistress, and begged
her to look after it and bring it up. And that's just
what she did – brought it up with every care and
attention, as if she were her own daughter – or as

117

*incestuous
name of
love →*

near as makes no difference.   55

Now, after she'd grown up and reached an age
where she became attractive to men, the old man
here (*points to the house again*) fell head over heels in
love with her – and so did his son, in fact! Now the
pair of them, father and son, are marshalling their
forces behind each other's back. The father has got
his bailiff to ask for the girl in marriage. He's
hoping, if the bailiff's lucky, he'll have found
himself somewhere to roost at night, away from
home, behind his wife's back! But the son has got
his servant to ask for the girl for himself; he knows,
if his servant is successful, he'll have the girl he
loves right on the spot, where he can get at her!

Now the old man's wife has found out that her
husband is up to no good, so she is siding with her
son. But the father, when he found out his son was
in love with the same girl, and might prove to be a
nuisance, packed him off abroad. So his mother,
using all her wits, is aiding his cause while he's
away. Don't expect the young man to come back to
the city today, during the course of this play –
because he won't! Plautus didn't want him to, so he
smashed down the bridge he'd have had to cross on
his way back!   79

I suppose there are some people here who are
saying: 'For goodness' sake, *what*'s this I hear?
Slaves getting married? Slaves taking wives, slaves
proposing marriage? *That*'s new – in fact it's quite
unheard of!' Well, *I* say it happens in Greece and at
Carthage, and here in our own country in Apulia;
it's normal there to make more fuss of a slave's
wedding than of a citizen's! And if anyone wants to
challenge that, he can bet me a jug of sweet wine –
so long as the referee's a Carthaginian, or a Greek,
that is – *or* an Apulian, for all I care! (*Pauses*) What?
No takers? I see – no one's thirsty!

(*Serious again*) Let me get back to this foundling
girl. This girl, the one the slaves are competing to
marry, will be found to be both freeborn *and* a

118

CASINA

virgin, the daughter of an Athenian citizen – so
she's not going to be doing any fornicating, not in
this play, anyway! (*More confidential*) Mind you,
later, after the show, I've an idea she'll take the
plunge without any of the formalities, if the offer's
right!   100

   That's all. Farewell, and good luck to you! May
you vanquish your enemies, and win your victory
with valour, as you have done before!

*Prologue goes off. Olympio (the old man's bailiff) and
Chalinus (the young man's servant) enter from the house of
Lysidamus.*

Olympio Can't I talk and think about my own affairs
without *you* spying on me? Why the devil are you
following me about like this?

Chalinus Because I've made up my mind to follow you like
your own shadow, wherever you go. Yes, even if
you go to hell, I'm coming with you! So work it out
for yourself; do you still think you can trick me and
carry off Casina as your wife?

Olympio (*airily*) What business can *you* have with *me*?

Chalinus (*indignant*) *What's* that, you scum? What are *you*
creeping about in the city for? Eh? A fine bailiff *you*
are!

Olympio Because I ... choose to.

Chalinus Why aren't you in the country, doing the job you're
meant to do? Why don't you do what you're sup-
posed to do, and stop meddling with city matters?
You've come here to make off with the girl I'm
going to marry! Get back to the country, where you
belong, and be quick about it!   122

Olympio I haven't forgotten my duty, Chalinus. I've left
someone in charge who can run things perfectly
well without me. And if I get what I came here for –
if I marry this girl you're so besotted with – the
luscious, the dainty little Casina who works with
you – I'll take her off to the country with me as my
bride, and *then* I'll sit tight where I belong – (*snig-
gering*) I'll be on the job *all* hours!

119

Chalinus *You* marry her? I'd rather ... *hang* myself than let you marry her!

Olympio The girl's mine, so you can go and put your head in the noose right away!

Chalinus She's yours, is she? You – dunghill-bred clod!

Olympio *You*'ll see.

Chalinus Oh, to blazes with you!

Olympio The ways I'm going to torture you at my wedding – you see if I don't!

Chalinus Oh? What do you have in mind?   140

Olympio You want to know? First of all, I'm going to make you carry a torch for the bride. Then, after the wedding, you'll be just the worthless good-for-nothing you've always been, and when you come out to the farm, you'll be given one jug, one path to walk, one spring, one pail, and eight damned great vats to fill! And if they're not kept topped up, I'll be doing some topping myself – with a whip! I'll have you so bent with carrying water you'll fit snugly round a horse's backside, like a crupper! What's more, when it comes to you wanting something to eat, you'll have to make do with a heap of cattle-fodder, or dirt, like an earth-worm – or else I'll make you so thin on that farm the word 'thin' won't even describe you! Then, when you're clapped out and starving, I'll see to it you get *just* the sort of sleeping accommodation you deserve!

Chalinus What d'you mean?   158

Olympio I'll have you tied up to the window-opening, so you can listen while I make love to Casina! And when she says to me 'My little love, Olympio dearest, love of my life, my honeybunch, joy of my soul, let me kiss those sweet eyes of yours, my heart's desire, do let me make love to you, *please*, O day of my delight, my little sparrow, my lovey-dovey, my darling *bunny*!' – while she's saying all this you'll be squirming about half way up the wall, you no-good, just like a cornered mouse!

Now I'm going inside. Don't feel you've got to say anything – I'm *sick* of talking to you!

Chalinus I'm coming too. You're not going to get up to
120

anything here without me knowing, I can tell you *that*!

Olympio and Chalinus go into the house. Cleostrata and her maid Pardalisca enter from Lysidamus's house.

Cleostrata   (*to maids inside*) Lock the larders, seal them up with sealing wax, and bring me back my signet ring. I'm just popping over here to my neighbour's house. If my husband wants me for anything, come over here for me.   177

Pardalisca   The master said he wanted lunch got ready.

Cleostrata   Shh! Hold your tongue, now – be off with you!
Pardalisca goes into the house.

I'm not getting it for him; there'll be no cooking today, not the way he's carrying on – fighting me and his own son in order to indulge himself – himself and his own ... filthy appetites – the *disgrace* that he is! But I'll punish him for it, the adulterer – he can go without food and drink! I'll nag him, call him dirty names, I'll treat him like dirt! Yes, I'll really give him the rough edge of my tongue and make him squirm. I'll give him just the sort of life he deserves, the silly old dodderer, the dirty old man, the filthy *beast*!

I'll go straight over to my neighbour's and tell her about my troubles. (*Hears a noise*) Wait a minute, there's someone at the door – ah, there she is coming out now. Oh dear, I didn't time my visit very well.

Myrrhina enters from Alcesimus's house.

Myrrhina   (*to slavegirls inside*) Come on, girls, come over here next door with me. (*Nothing happens*) Hullo? Isn't anyone listening to what I say?
Maids appear.

I'll be over here (*pointing*) if my husband or anyone else wants me ... When I'm alone at home I get so tired my hands just won't do the work! ... Didn't I tell you to bring me a distaff?   201

Cleostrata   (*stepping towards her*) Myrrhina, good morning!

Myrrhina   (*seeing her*) Oh! Good morning. (*Seeing her face*)

121

	What's the matter? Why are you so upset?
Cleostrata	(*heaving a sigh*) Oh, it's quite normal for women with unhappy marriages to get upset – there's always something to upset them, indoors and out. I was just coming over to your place.
Myrrhina	Well, and I was just coming over to you!... But tell me, what's making you so miserable? When you're unhappy it makes me unhappy too!
Cleostrata	Yes – I really do believe it does! I don't know a neighbour I'm more fond of than you – and rightly, too. There's no one I admire more, either!
Myrrhina	I'm fond of you, too – and I really do want to know what's the matter.
Cleostrata	It's ... the awful way I'm ... treated at home!
Myrrhina	Oh dear, *what*'s that? Tell me again, will you? I'm not quite clear what it is you're complaining about.
Cleostrata	It's my husband – he really treats me like dirt! It's no good standing up for my rights – I haven't a chance! 222
Myrrhina	That's strange, if it's true – it's usually men who complain their wives won't give them what's theirs by rights!
Cleostrata	Do you know, there's this serving girl I've got. I brought her up at my own expense, and he wants to ride roughshod over me and marry her to his bailiff – but the truth of the matter is, he's fallen for her himself.
Myrrhina	(*looking around anxiously*) Shh! For goodness' sake!
Cleostrata	But surely we can talk here – we're alone!
Myrrhina	(*calmer*) Yes, I suppose you're right. (*Frowning*) But how *can* she be yours? No decent woman should have property behind her husband's back – and if she has, she hasn't come by it any proper way. She's either stolen it from her husband, or got it from a lover. As I see it, everything you own is your husband's property.
Cleostrata	(*taking umbrage*) There! We're friends and everything you say is *against* me! 241
Myrrhina	Shh! You silly goose, listen to me. Don't stand in your husband's way; so long as he sees you're well

	provided for at home, *let* him have his love affair!
Cleostrata	Are you crazy? How can that be in any wife's interest?
Myrrhina	You fool! There's one thing you *never* want to hear your husband say – at any cost.
Cleostrata	What's that?
Myrrhina	'Pack your bags, woman; clear out!'
Cleostrata	Shh! Quiet!
Myrrhina	What's the matter?
Cleostrata	Look!
Myrrhina	Whom can you see?
Cleostrata	It's my husband coming. In you go, please, hurry up!

Cleostrata pushes Myrrhina back towards her own house.

Myrrhina	All right, I'm coming. (*Stands in her own doorway*)
Cleostrata	Later on, when we've both got more time to spare, I'll come and talk things over. 'Bye for now!
Myrrhina	Goodbye! 260

Myrrhina goes in. Lysidamus enters in high spirits. He does not see Cleostrata at first.

Lysidamus
Ah love, *sweet* love! Can anything
Quite match its sparkle? No, I'm sure
For charm, for magic, and for fun
There's nothing like it in the world!
It has a spice all of its own –
In fact, I wonder cooks, who use
All sorts of flavourings, can do
Without the king of condiments!
If love is there to give it spice
What meal could fail to please a man?
What food has any decent taste,
Whether it's salt or sweet, if love's
Not one of the ingredients?
For love can make the bitterest thing
Seem sweet as honey, make the boor
A smiling charmer overnight!
Now I'm not passing on what I've
Heard other people saying – no;

123

I've learnt the truth of this myself!
Now I'm in love with Casina,   280
Well – look at how I've blossomed out!
I'm the last word in elegance!
I'm in and out the perfume shops,
And if I find a special scent
I'll wear it just for *her*. I want
Her to be fond of me, and – do
You know? – I really think she is! (*Pause*)

(*Coming down to earth*) But there's my wife – she really torments me, just by living and breathing! There she is, standing there with that permanent scowl on her face. She's a *disaster*! But I'd better say something, just to butter her up. (*Goes over to her*) And how are you, my darling wife?

Cleostrata	Get away – and don't touch me!
Lysidamus	Now, now! Don't be so sour. Is that the way for my Juno to talk to her Jove? – Where are you rushing off to?
Cleostrata	Leave me alone!
Lysidamus	No, wait!
Cleostrata	I won't! 300
Lysidamus	Well, I'll follow you, then.
Cleostrata	Have you gone mad?
Lysidamus	Only mad with love for you!
Cleostrata	I don't *want* your love.
Lysidamus	I'm sorry, you've got it! (*Tries to embrace her*)
Cleostrata	(*struggling*) No, no! I'd rather die!
Lysidamus	(*aside*) If only you meant that! I wish you did!
Cleostrata	(*overhearing*) Yes, I'm sure you do.
Lysidamus	(*aloud*) Just look at me, my sweet, *please*?
Cleostrata	Your 'sweet'? Oh yes, about as much as you are mine! (*Suddenly sniffing*) Where's that smell of perfume coming from, eh?
Lysidamus	(*aside*) Oh my god! Oh help! Caught in the act! I'll have to use my cloak and wipe it off. (*He tries to*) Damn that perfumer for selling it to me in the first place!
Cleostrata	Oh! You good-for-nothing, you grey-haired old *goat*

124

	– it's all I can do to stop myself telling you a few home truths about yourself! A man at your time of life parading about the streets drenched in perfume – oh, you useless lump! 321
Lysidamus	Look, I promise, I've been helping a friend shop for some perfumes.
Cleostrata	What a ready tongue he has! (*Turning on him*) Haven't you *any* sense of shame?
Lysidamus	(*cowed*) Yes, of course, dear – whatever you say, dear.
Cleostrata	Where have you been wallowing, eh? What bawdy house?
Lysidamus	Me? In a *bawdy house*?
Cleostrata	I know more than you think.
Lysidamus	(*alarmed*) Eh? What's that? What do you know?
Cleostrata	That – you're the most useless old fool in creation, that's what. Where have you been, you good-for-nothing? Where have you been drinking? So help me, you're *drunk*! Look how crumpled your cloak is!
Lysidamus	God strike me down – no *both* of us! – if so much as a drop of wine has passed my lips today!
Cleostrata	Oh, don't mind me – do as you please – drink, stuff yourself, run us all into debt! 340
Lysidamus	Now, stop! That's quite enough, woman. Control yourself! That's more than enough of your yapping. Leave yourself something to nag me about tomorrow... (*Pauses*) Now tell me: have you managed to get a grip on yourself? Are you ready to do what your husband wants, instead of fighting him all the time?
Cleostrata	Well, what is it?
Lysidamus	As if you didn't know! It concerns our maid Casina – is she going to be married to our bailiff Olympio? He's a decent servant, and she'll have a nice house, with plenty of wood, hot water, food and clothes, where she can bring up her children. I don't want her to marry that worthless slave, that ne'er-do-well soldier's lackey Chalinus – why, he hasn't got a brass farthing saved up of his own!
Cleostrata	Heavens, you really surprise me, forgetting the way

125

	to behave – and you at your time of life, too!
Lysidamus	What do you mean? 359
Cleostrata	Well, if you were doing the right and proper thing, you'd let me look after the maids myself – they're my province, after all.
Lysidamus	But why the devil do you want to give her to a mere ... shield-carrier type?
Cleostrata	Why? Because we both ought to be supporting our only son, that's why!
Lysidamus	Only son he may be – but no more than I'm his only father! If there's any standing down to be done, he ought to be doing it for me, rather than the other way round!
Cleostrata	My dear Lysidamus, you really are looking for trouble!
Lysidamus	(*aside*) She can smell something fishy – I know it! (*Aloud*) Me? M-m-me?
Cleostrata	Yes, you! What are you stammering for?... Why are you so *set* on that wedding, eh?
Lysidamus	Oh, it's just that I'd rather a decent servant got the girl than a dishonest one.
Cleostrata	What if I work on the bailiff and get him to give her up for the orderly? 380
Lysidamus	And what if I work on the orderly and get him to give her up for the bailiff? I think I could, too!
Cleostrata	All right. You want me to call Chalinus out here? You reason with him, and I'll reason with the bailiff.
Lysidamus	By all means, yes.
Cleostrata	(*turning to go*) He'll be out in a moment. We'll soon see which of us is better at persuasion!

Cleostrata goes out.

Lysidamus	(*waiting until she has gone*) *Damn* the bloody woman! (*Looks round nervously*) Whew! Nice to be able to get *that* off my chest! Oh God – here's me, suffering all the tortures of the damned with this love of mine, and *she* seems to go out of her way to thwart me! No, she must've got wind of what I'm up to – that's why she's so set on helping the orderly.

Chalinus enters from the house, unseen by Lysidamus.

Damn the man, confound him, *curse* him!

Chalinus (*superciliously*) Your wife said you wanted me.

Lysidamus That's right. I did tell her to fetch you out.

Chalinus Well, what do you want, then?   399

Lysidamus First of all, I'd like to see you adopt a more respectful attitude when you talk to me. It's ridiculous for you to be so surly to a superior. I've always thought of you as a decent, honest sort of fellow.

Chalinus I see. Well, if you feel that way, why not give me my freedom, eh?

Lysidamus I want to do just that, I really do! But my wanting to is no use if you don't back me up yourself . . . in a practical way, I mean.

Chalinus Just tell me what you want – that's what I'd like to know.

Lysidamus Listen then, and I'll tell you. I promised young Casina to our bailiff.

Chalinus Yes, but your wife and son have promised her to *me*.

Lysidamus I know. But which would you prefer – to stay single and to be a free man, or live the rest of your life a slave, you and your children after you? Those are the alternatives – you can take your pick.

Chalinus If I was free, I'd have to support myself. As it is, you support me. No – I'm certainly not giving up Casina, not to anyone I won't.   420

Lysidamus (*angrily*) Right. In you go and call my wife out here straight away. And bring an urn of water with you – and the lots.[2]

Chalinus All right. Suits me.

Lysidamus A conspiracy, by God! Well, one way or another, I'll scotch it! If I can't get my way by persuasion, I'll settle it by the lots. I'll get my own back on you and those cronies of yours!

Chalinus Oh, no you won't – because I'm going to draw the winning lot!

Lysidamus And your prize is going to be protracted and painful!

Chalinus You can scheme as much as you like, Casina's going to marry me!

127

Lysidamus	Oh, get out of my sight!
Chalinus	(*cheekily*) You don't seem to enjoy my company much – but I'll survive. 437

Chalinus goes inside.

Lysidamus Well, things can't get much worse than this! Everything's against me today! And supposing my wife's persuaded Olympio to give up Casina! If she has, well, say goodbye, Lysidamus!... But if she hasn't, on the other hand, there's still a ray of hope ... there's still the lots. And if even that comes to nothing – (*suddenly tragic*) well, I shall take my sword for a bed – and fall upon it!

The door opens.

Ah, good! Here comes Olympio!

Olympio comes out of the house.

Olympio (*to Cleostrata inside*) No, ma'am, the answer's *no*! You can put me in a red-hot oven and bake me black as burnt bread – but you're wasting your time, you won't get me to do what you want!

Lysidamus I'm saved, then! That must mean there's still hope!

Olympio Why are you trying to scare me with all that talk about setting me free? Whether you like it or not, ma'am, despite the pair of you, however much you object, you *or* your son, I can have my freedom for next to nothing!

Lysidamus What's all this, Olympio? Who are you arguing with?

Olympio The one you're always arguing with.

Lysidamus My wife? 460

Olympio 'Wife', is she? Huh! You're more like a huntsman than a husband – always got a bitch at your heels, day in, day out!

Lysidamus What's she up to? What has she said to you?

Olympio She's been on and on at me, begging me not to marry Casina.

Lysidamus Well, what did you say?

Olympio I said I wouldn't give her up if Jove Almighty asked me!

Lysidamus (*jubilantly*) *Bless* you, Olympio! *Bless* you!

Olympio	Now she's all huffed up, she's *bursting* with anger at me!
Lysidamus	She can split right down the middle for all I care!
Olympio	She has already, surely, if you've done your stuff as a husband! But really, this love affair of yours is getting me down. Your wife hates me, your son hates me – the whole household hates me!
Lysidamus	What does it matter to you? So long as Jupiter here (*pats himself*) is on your side, you can forget all the lesser gods! 480
Olympio	Now, that's a lot of nonsense. You know perfectly well how your human Jupiters suddenly die off – well, if you die and your kingdom passes into the hands of these lesser gods, who's going to look after my hide for me then? Who'll be around to save my neck?
Lysidamus	Look – if we work it so I can sleep with Casina, you'll be better off than you think.
Olympio	Well, I just don't think it's possible: your wife's absolutely determined I shan't have her.
Lysidamus	No, I've got a plan – listen: I'm going to throw the lots into an urn and draw them out for you and Chalinus. The way things have turned out I reckon we'll have to change tactics and get down to fighting in real earnest!
Olympio	What if the lots don't come out the way you want?
Lysidamus	Don't even *think* such things! I'm trusting to heaven – we'll rest our hopes in heaven.
Olympio	Hm! I wouldn't give you tuppence for your hopes in heaven! Everyone trusts in heaven – but I've seen heaven-trusters looking foolish often enough, plenty of 'em! 502
Lysidamus	(*suddenly listening*) Sh! Quiet a moment!
Olympio	Why?
Lysidamus	Look – there's Chalinus coming out with the urn and lots. Now we'll do battle and decide it one way or the other!

Chalinus enters with an urn and lots: Cleostrata follows him.

129

Cleostrata	Well, Chalinus, what does my husband want?
Chalinus	To see you burning on your bier outside the city gates, if you ask me!
Cleostrata	Yes, I really believe he does.
Chalinus	Believe it? I know it for a fact!
Lysidamus	(*to Olympio*) Well, I've more talent in my household than I thought: this fellow here's a mind-reader! (*Assuming his military air again*) Now then – up standards and advance! Let's engage them! Follow me! (*To Cleostrata and Chalinus*) What are you two up to?
Chalinus	Everything you wanted is here – wife, lots, urn – and me. 520
Olympio	If you're here there's one too many for my taste!
Chalinus	But that's just *your* taste. And why? Because I'm here to needle you – to keep on poking you in your dear little ribs! You useless oaf, you're already in a cold sweat!
Lysidamus	Quiet, Chalinus!
Chalinus	Make him shut up! *Force* him!
Olympio	No – force *him*. He *likes* it (*sniggering*) – he's used to it, after all!
Lysidamus	(*to Chalinus*) Put the urn down here: give me the lots. Now pay attention, both of you. (*To Cleostrata, making a last effort*) This is a pity, my dear – I did think I could get you to let me marry Casina – in fact, I still think there's a chance.
Cleostrata	*You* marry Casina?
Lysidamus	Yes, me ... oh dear, *no* – that wasn't what I meant to say ... er, when I said 'me', I meant 'him', er ... and I was so anxious to get her – no, to say it ... oh God, what a lot of nonsense I've been talking! 540
Cleostrata	And still are!
Lysidamus	... let *him* ... no, no, let *me*, dammit – (*collects himself at last*) ah, at *last*, I'm back on the right track!
Cleostrata	You do enough straying from it, I must say!
Lysidamus	Well, that happens when you're anxious about something ... But ... out of consideration for your

rights in the matter ... Olympio and I – both of us – are *appealing* to you.

Cleostrata To do what?

Lysidamus Er, just this, my dearest – *please* will you give in to our bailiff here over Casina – just as a favour?

Cleostrata I certainly will not. I wouldn't *dream* of it!

Lysidamus Right, then. I'm for handing out the lots to the two of them without more ado.

Cleostrata Who's stopping you?

Lysidamus (*blandly*) Yes, this seems the best and fairest way, in my considered opinion. Then, if it turns out the way we want, we'll be delighted; and if it doesn't, we'll have to grin and bear it. Now (*to Olympio*) here's your lot. What's written on it?[3]   561

Olympio A one.

Chalinus That's not fair! Why should *he* get it first?

Lysidamus Here, you take this one.

Chalinus Give it here!

Olympio Here – wait a moment, I've just had a thought. (*To Lysidamus*) Take a look and see there's not *another* lot under the water there!

Chalinus You cheeky – ! Think we're *all* like you, do you?

Lysidamus There isn't any; just relax!

Chalinus (*getting ready to drop it into the water*) Here goes, then (*raises hands in prayer*), and I hope to heaven it brings me luck!

Olympio You'll get luck, all right – bad luck! I know what heaven thinks of you! Wait a moment, though – that lot of yours – it's not of poplar or fir, is it?

Chalinus What's it to you?

Olympio Well, I don't want it floating on the top of the water.   579

Lysidamus Yes! That's a thought! Keep your eyes on it! (*Goes to the side of the urn*) Now, both of you, throw your lots in here.

Olympio and Chalinus throw in their lots.

There they go! You see everything's done fairly, Cleostrata dear!

Olympio I wouldn't trust your wife if I was you!

Lysidamus Relax!

Olympio	I can't! She'll lay a bloody spell on those lots, soon as she gets hold of them!
Lysidamus	Quiet!
Olympio	I am. (*Raises his hands in prayer*) I hope to heaven –
Chalinus	– you'll carry a ball and chain before the day's out!
Olympio	– that I have the luck –
Chalinus	– of being hung up by your heels!
Olympio	No! Of wiping the floor with you so hard I wipe you right out!
	Chalinus starts at his vehemence.
	What are you so scared of, eh? You might as well get ready to do yourself in! You're finished!
Lysidamus	Pay attention, both of you.
Olympio	I'm not saying a thing. 599
Lysidamus	Now, Cleostrata – so you can't claim I tricked you over this, or suspect me of anything – I'm handing it over to you. *You* do the drawing.
Olympio	That's the end of *me*, then!
Chalinus	He's better off, then! (*Gesturing at Lysidamus*)
Cleostrata	(*to Lysidamus*) Thank you.
Chalinus	(*sneering at Olympio*) I hope to heaven – your lot jumps out of the urn and gets lost!
Olympio	Oh yes? Just because *you*'re the low sort of slave who does a bunk, you expect to set the fashion, do you?
Chalinus	I hope your lot just melts away to nothing, like in the story of the Heraclidae.[4]
Olympio	You'll melt away yourself shortly – you'll be so warmed by the whiplash!
Lysidamus	Olympio, pay attention.
Olympio	I would, if the professor here would let me!
Lysidamus	(*as Cleostrata prepares to draw*) Heaven bring me luck!
Olympio	Yes – and me!
Chalinus	No – me!
Olympio	No, no – me! 620
Chalinus	No, dammit, *me*!
Cleostrata	(*to Olympio*) He'll win (*pointing at Chalinus*) and you'll get what's coming to you.
Lysidamus	(*to Olympio*) Punch his face in! Go on, let's have some action!

132

Cleostrata	(*to Olympio*) Don't you dare touch him!
Olympio	(*to Lysidamus*) What, a slap, do you mean – or a real punch?
Lysidamus	Suit yourself.
Olympio	(*hits Chalinus*) There, take that!
Cleostrata	(*angrily*) What did you do that for?
Olympio	Orders, ma'am – from Jupiter here!
Cleostrata	(*to Chalinus*) Hit him back on the face – tit for tat!
Olympio	Ouch! He's beating me to pulp, Jupiter, sir!
Lysidamus	(*to Chalinus*) What did you do that for?
Chalinus	Orders, sir – from Juno here!
Lysidamus	Well, I suppose I must put up with it. In my house it's the wife who gives the orders.
Cleostrata	Chalinus has the same right to speak as your man.
Olympio	Why does he muck up all my prayers, eh? 640
Lysidamus	Chalinus, you look out – I'm warning you!
Chalinus	Now he tells me – *after* I've had my face punched in!
Lysidamus	(*to Cleostrata*) Come on, dear – now draw the lots. You two, pay attention. (*Aside*) I'm so on edge I don't even know where I am! Oh my god, I'm going to have a heart attack – it's been jumping about for ages now – giving my chest the most *awful* hammering!
Cleostrata	(*feeling in the urn*) I've got one!
Lysidamus	Bring it out!
Cleostrata	(*grimly*) This is it!
Olympio	Let's see it!
	Cleostrata holds the lot up.
	It's *mine*! It's *mine*!
Chalinus	It's misery – *that*'s what it is!
Cleostrata	(*sadly*) You've lost, Chalinus.
Lysidamus	(*jubilantly*) Well, Olympio, congratulations! The gods were on our side!
Olympio	Yes, it's because of the pious life I've led – my fore-fathers were just the same – it's in the family. 660
Lysidamus	(*to Cleostrata*) Go inside now, dear, and get everything ready for the wedding.
Cleostrata	(*absently*) I will, yes.
Lysidamus	(*in a hurry*) You do know, don't you, it's a long way

133

CASINA

out to the villa in the country where he's to take the bride?

Cleostrata Yes.

Lysidamus Well, go in and see to everything, then. I know this isn't to your liking – but do it just the same!

Cleostrata All right.

Cleostrata goes inside her house.

Lysidamus (*to Olympio*) Why don't we go inside, too, and hurry them up?

Olympio Why don't we? Come on! 673

Lysidamus (*confidentially*) I don't want to discuss it any further while *he*'s (*nods at Chalinus*) around within earshot.

Lysidamus and Olympio go inside. Chalinus is left in high dudgeon.

Chalinus If I went straight off and hanged myself, I'd just have wasted my time – *and* there's the expense of the rope to take into consideration – *and* all the satisfaction I'd give my enemies! Anyway, what's the point? I'm half dead as it is! Ah well, the lots went against me – Casina's marrying the bailiff. I don't mind so much that the bailiff won – but what does annoy me is the way the old man was so determined *I* shouldn't have her, and he *should*. What a stew he got in, what a panic! The way he was leaping about when the bailiff won! Aha! (*listening*) I can hear the door opening – I'll just stand back here (*retiring backstage*) – those two dear friends of mine are coming out! I'll stay hidden here and listen in to what they say. 690

Olympio and Lysidamus come out.

Olympio Chalinus? Just let him come out to the farm! I'll send him back home to the city like a charcoal-seller, with his neck in a sling!

Lysidamus So you should.

Olympio I'll see to it – leave it to me.

Lysidamus If he was around, I'd have liked to send Chalinus

134

off with you to shop for some food – he! he! – just to rub salt into the blighter's wounds!

Chalinus (*aside*) I'll sidle back up against the wall here, like a crab ... I *must* listen in to what they're saying. One's sticking the knife in my back – the other's turning it! Just look at our bridegroom (*nods at Olympio*) swaggering about, all dressed in white – the rotten bastard, the dirty low-down crook! No – I'm putting off my suicide – I've decided to send him down to Hades first!   706

Olympio Well now, what a useful fellow I've turned out to be! You've got what you wanted most in the world – and it's all due to me! Today you'll be together with your lady love at last, and your wife knows nothing about it!

Lysidamus (*glances at the door*) Shhh! (*Deliriously*) In view of all you've done for me, bless me, it's as much as I can do to stop myself showering kisses on you – my *dearest* boy!

Chalinus (*aside*) Eh? 'Showering kisses'? *What*'s this? Your 'dearest boy'? Blow me down, I think the old boy's about to make love to the fellow!

Olympio You're fond of me now, then are you?

Lysidamus Fond? Why, I love you more than I love myself! Here – may I ... let me *embrace* you!   721

Chalinus (*aside*) *Eh?* Embrace him?

Olympio If you like.

Lysidamus (*hugging and kissing him*) Oh, when I hold you in my arms like this, it's like lapping honey!

Olympio (*pushing Lysidamus away*) Hey, get off! Off my back, you old goat!

Chalinus (*aside*) That's *it*! That's why he made him his bailiff! *Yes*, and some time ago when I went to bring him home from a party, he tried to promote me to steward – right on the doorstep there!

Olympio Yes, I really did do you a good turn today! You must have been tickled pink!

Lysidamus Yes, and believe me, as long as I live, I'll look after you second to none.

Chalinus Damn me, I reckon these two'll be hard at it in a

	moment! The old boy goes for the hairy types, obviously! 738
Lysidamus	Oh, the kissing Casina's going to get tonight! – the time I'm going to have behind the old girl's back!
Chalinus	(*aside, triumphantly*) Aha! *Now* I see – good Lord yes, *now* I'm on the right track! It's the old man – he's fallen for Casina himself! I've *got* the blighter!
Lysidamus	God, how I ache to hold her in my arms, to kiss her!
Olympio	Let's get her married first. What's the mad rush for, dammit?
Lysidamus	I'm in *love*!
Olympio	Well, I don't think it can be managed today.
Lysidamus	Oh yes it can – if you reckon on being a free man tomorrow!
Chalinus	(*aside*) Wow! I must listen into this even more closely! I'll be killing two birds with one stone – pretty neat!
Lysidamus	I've got a place to go – at my friend and neighbour's here. (*Points to the house of Alcesimus*) I've told him all about this affair of mine, and he said he'd give me somewhere to go. 757
Olympio	What about his wife? Where's she going to be?
Lysidamus	Ah, I've hit on a really clever idea there. My wife will invite her over to our place for the wedding – you know, to keep her company, help her, and spend the night with her. I've suggested she does that, and my wife agreed. Myrrhina is going to sleep at our house, and I'll make sure Alcesimus is out of the house, too. You'll take your bride off to the farm – but the farm's going to be here – at least while I'm bedding down with Casina! Then you'll take her back to the country before daylight tomorrow. Neat, eh?
Olympio	Clever, yes.
Chalinus	(*aside*) That's right – you do all the scheming you like! You'll pay for being such a pair of clever dicks, though – damme if you won't!
Lysidamus	Now I've got a job for you.
Olympio	Yes?
Lysidamus	Take this purse and go and buy some food. Go on,

	get a move on – but make it something special, mind – something really mouth-watering – as luscious as Casina herself!
Olympio	All right.
Lysidamus	Get some baby cuttlefish, limpets, squid, fish-cakes –
Chalinus	*(aside)* Ugh! *Fruit* cake would be better! I hate fish.
Lysidamus	– and soles –
Chalinus	*(aside)* Yes, why not wooden ones, to kick your teeth in with, you dirty old man!
Olympio	What about dog-fish?
Lysidamus	What's the point? I've got my wife at home. She's all the bitch-fish I need – she never shuts up!
Olympio	Well, when I'm there, I can decide what to buy from all the fish on display.
Lysidamus	Fair enough. Off you go. Don't worry about the expense – get plenty of everything... Well, I'd better see my neighbour over here and make sure he takes care of his side of the bargain.
Olympio	Shall I go, then?
Lysidamus	Yes, off you go.

780

797

Olympio goes off to the Forum, Lysidamus into his neighbour's house.

| | |
| **Chalinus** | My God, I'm going to land that pair in it! I'm going to tell my mistress the whole story right away! I wouldn't miss this for *anything* – not for my freedom three times over! I've caught my enemies red-handed, I've got 'em in the act! If my mistress is willing to do her bit now, we've *won* – the case is open and shut! I'm going to be smart, I'll steal a march on both of them! *(Dramatically)* The omens are on our side today! The lovers' luck has changed!... I'm off inside now... Those two have cooked up something, all right, but I'm going to give it a quite different flavour! They won't have quite the party they planned – but they'll be getting a reception, all right – planned by *me*! |

Chalinus goes into the house. Lysidamus and Alcesimus come out of Alcesimus's house.

137

Lysidamus	Here's where I find out whether you're a real friend or not, Alcesimus; now you'll show your true colours, now's the testing time. If you're going to take me to task for having this affair, don't bother. All that stuff about 'with your grey hair' and 'at your time of life' – you can save it! 'A married man like you!' – that's something else you can keep, too.
Alcesimus	(*amused*) I certainly never set eyes on a man more lovesick than you! 820
Lysidamus	Please make sure your house is empty.
Alcesimus	Don't worry! I've already decided – I'm sending all the slaves and maidservants over to your place.
Lysidamus	(*overjoyed*) Oh good man, what a good idea! But remember the blackbird's advice: see they come over 'with all the food they can find'[5] – and at the double, too, as if their lives depended on it!
Alcesimus	I'll remember.
Lysidamus	Splendid! My friend, you're more astute than a statute! Look after things, will you? I'm off to the Forum, but I'll be right back.
Alcesimus	Enjoy yourself.
Lysidamus	While I'm gone, give your house some speech therapy, will you?
Alcesimus	Eh? Why should I do that?
Lysidamus	So it can give me a decent welcome when I get back! – An *empty* welcome!
Alcesimus	Ouch! You need slapping down – you're getting far too full of yourself! 839
Lysidamus	What's the point of being in love if I'm not witty and clever with it? (*Turning to go*) Now don't get lost so I have to go looking for you!
Alcesimus	I shan't set foot outside my house.

They go off, Lysidamus to the Forum, stage left, Alcesimus into his house. Cleostrata comes out of her house.

Cleostrata	*Well!* That was why my husband was so insistent I should hurry and invite my neighbour over to our house – he wanted to have the house empty so they

138

could take Casina there! Well, now I'm *not* going to ask her over – no, that's the *last* thing I'm going to do, give them somewhere to monkey about in just as they like, the dirty devils, the pathetic old *eunuchs*!

Alcesimus comes out.

Ah, here he comes, that pillar of the Senate, that champion of the people, my dear neighbour Alcesimus – who's giving my husband the run of his house for his philandering! *Huh!* He's not worth a pinch of salt, that one!

Alcesimus	It's strange my wife hasn't been asked next door yet. She's been dressed up and waiting to be called for ages now! Ah, here's our neighbour coming to get her, I suppose. Good day to you, Cleostrata!
Cleostrata	And to you, Alcesimus. Where's your wife? 861
Alcesimus	Inside, waiting for you to fetch her. Er ... your husband asked me to send her over to your place to help you. Do you want me to call her?
Cleostrata	No, don't disturb her. Don't bother if she's busy.
Alcesimus	(*anxiously*) But she isn't!
Cleostrata	Never mind, I don't want to be a nuisance. I'll see her later.
Alcesimus	Aren't you getting ready for the wedding over at your place?
Cleostrata	Yes – everything's under control.
Alcesimus	(*shaken*) Er ... don't you need someone to help you?
Cleostrata	No. There's plenty of help at home. When the wedding's over, I'll come and see her. Goodbye, now, and give her my love!

Cleostrata leaves front of stage but does not go off.

Alcesimus What am I going to do now? ... I'm in this filthy business up to the neck, dammit ... and all because of that dirty, toothless old ram Lysidamus! It was his fault – he dragged me into this. I go and promise my wife's help next door, too, as if she's some sort of dishwasher! The rotten liar, saying his wife was coming over to fetch mine – and *she* tells me she doesn't need her at all!... Now, *wait* a moment – I wonder if our neighbour can have got wind of this business already!... Yes! ... but no, on second thoughts, if it was anything like that she'd have tackled me about it, surely... I'm going inside... I'd better haul the old girl back to her berth in dry dock! 890

Alcesimus goes in.

Cleostrata (*emerging from her doorway*) Haha! That fooled him good and proper! What a panic the old fool was in! Now, I'd just like that worthless, clapped-out old husband of mine to put in an appearance, so I could make a fool of him, too. I've had my fun with his friend Alcesimus here; it's *his* turn now! I'm really itching to set the two of them at each other's throats! (*Looks down the street*) Here he comes, too! To look at that earnest expression on his face, you'd think he was ... respectable! 900

Cleostrata retires again into the doorway. Lysidamus returns from the Forum, stage left, in a peeved and irritable mood.

Lysidamus It really is idiotic, the way I see it, for a man in love to choose the very day he has a sweetheart ready and waiting for him to go off to the Forum! And that's just what I did – stupid fool that I am! I've wasted the day acting as counsellor to a relative of mine. He lost his case, too – and I'm *delighted*! Serve him right for calling on *me* to help him today! To my way of thinking, if a man calls on someone for legal assistance, he ought to ask him first and see if his *mind's* on the job or not; and if he says it's *not*, he should send him off home! An *absent*-minded counsellor's no use at all to him! (*Suddenly seeing Cleostrata*) Oh, there's my wife in front of the house! Oh my god, she's not deaf – she must have heard everything I've said!

Cleostrata (*aside*) I heard, all right, and you'll regret it, too!

Lysidamus	(*aside*) I'll go and speak to her. (*Aloud*) Well, my little bundle of joy, and what are *you* up to?
Cleostrata	I was waiting for you, actually.
Lysidamus	Is everything fixed? Have you got your neighbour over here to help you with things? 921
Cleostrata	I called for her, just as you told me to, but your great friend and partner Alcesimus was furious with her for some reason. When I asked her over he said he couldn't possibly let her come!
Lysidamus	(*disturbed*) That's your greatest failing – you don't know how to *charm* people.
Cleostrata	It's not for a wife to make up to other people's husbands, *dear* – that's a tart's business! You go over and call for her yourself; I ought to go and see if anything needs doing inside – *dear*.
Lysidamus	Well, hurry up.
Cleostrata	All right. (*Aside*) I'll really put the wind up him now! I'll make him the most miserable philanderer on god's earth before the day's out!

Cleostrata goes in. Alcesimus comes out of his house.

Alcesimus	I thought I'd come out and see if lover-boy's got back from the Forum yet – the old *scarecrow*, making fools of me and my wife like this! Ah, there he is, in front of the house! (*To Lysidamus*) There's a coincidence! I was just coming to find you! 940
Lysidamus	Yes, I wanted you, too. What have you got to say for yourself, you useless fool – what did I tell you to do? What did I *beg* you to do for me, eh?
Alcesimus	Well, what *was* it?
Lysidamus	(*ironically*) What a splendid job you made of it all – placing your house at my disposal and taking your wife across to our place! Well, I hope you're satisfied! So much for me and my big chance – and it's all your fault!
Alcesimus	Oh, to hell with you! Didn't you say your wife was going to come and ask my wife over? Of course you did!
Lysidamus	Yes. She says she did ask her over – and you said you weren't going to let her come!

141

Alcesimus	Well, *she* told me she didn't need her!
Lysidamus	Well, she's sent *me* to ask her over now!
Alcesimus	Well, I really couldn't care less!
Lysidamus	Well, you're *destroying* me, man!
Alcesimus	Well, that's *splendid*! Well now, I'm going to keep you waiting a long time yet! Well, well, I really am *itching* to – 961
Lysidamus	Well, but –
Alcesimus	– to cut you down to size!
Lysidamus	Well, and *I*'ll do the same for *you*, with the greatest of pleasure! You're not going to get in more 'well's than me! Never!
Alcesimus	Well, you can go to hell, once and for all, and make an end of it!
Lysidamus	*Well*, now – are you going to send your wife over to my place or not?
Alcesimus	You take her, and to hell with the whole lot of you – you, your wife, my wife, and that mistress of yours, too! (*Calming down*) Yes, you go, don't worry about that. I'll tell her to go through the garden straight away to see your wife.
Lysidamus	(*elated*) Now you're being a real friend to me! *Alcesimus goes in.* I wonder what evil omen crossed my path when I got mixed up in this affair! What harm did I ever do Venus to be in love and have everything conspiring to frustrate me like this? (*Starts*) Good Lord! What's that awful noise I can hear in the house?

The maid Pardalisca comes out of the house in a terrible fright.

Pardalisca	(*mock tragically*)

I'm done for, done for! I'm as good as dead! 982
My heart's stopped beating I'm so petrified!
My body's shaking like a leaf with fear!
I'm so afraid, I don't know where to turn!
Where shall I look for safety or for help?
Where can I run for refuge? – I don't *know*!
I've never seen the like of it before –
What I've just seen inside – I never did!

142

Such goings-on, such *temper* on display!

(*Calling inside*) Keep clear of her, ma'am, for heaven's sake watch out! She's mad with rage, she could do you a mischief! She's out of her mind – get that sword away from her!

Lysidamus	(*aside*) Lord, what *can* the matter be? Tearing out here like this, half dead with fright! (*Aloud*) Pardalisca!
Pardalisca	(*still tragic*) Ah me! Whence came that sound which fills my ears?
Lysidamus	I'm over here. *This* way. 1000
Pardalisca	Oh, *master*!
Lysidamus	What's the matter? Why are you so frightened?
Pardalisca	It's all up with me – and you, too!
Lysidamus	Eh? Me? All up with *me*? Why?
Pardalisca	I pity you, really I do!
Lysidamus	Save your pity for yourself.
Pardalisca	Oh, hold me, please, before I drop! (*Swoons*)
Lysidamus	(*steadying her*) Whatever it is, you'd better tell me quick.
Pardalisca	(*weakly*) Put an arm round my waist – oh, air, *please*, use your cloak and fan me!
Lysidamus	(*aside*) I don't like the sound of this – unless perhaps she's had a little too much neat wine somewhere and it's gone to her head.
Pardalisca	(*enjoying herself*) Please hold me by the ears!
Lysidamus	Oh, get off me and stop it! Damn you – waist, ears, head, and all! If you don't hurry up and tell me what all this is about, I'll brain you with this stick of mine, you viper. You've been making a fool of me all along, you little bitch! 1020
Pardalisca	Master – !
Lysidamus	(*ironically*) Well, now, my dear girl, what *is* it?
Pardalisca	You're not being fair to me!
Lysidamus	You haven't seen *anything* yet! But, come on, tell me what's the matter – and make it quick. What was all that commotion inside?
Pardalisca	I'll *tell* you if you'll listen. It was *awful*, really *awful* in there just now – the way your maid was career-

	ing about the house – well, hardly the way for an Athenian girl to behave!
Lysidamus	What's this?
Pardalisca	My tongue – I'm so scared, it's *paralysed*!
Lysidamus	(*impatiently*) Look, are you going to tell me what's up or not?
Pardalisca	Yes. Your serving girl – the one you want to marry to your bailiff – well, just now, inside –
Lysidamus	*Well?* What did she *do* in there?
Pardalisca	She's behaving just like one of those wicked Danaïd women in the legend – threatening her own husband! His life – 1040
Lysidamus	Eh? What did she threaten to do?
Pardalisca	(*shocked*) Ahhh!
Lysidamus	Well, *what?*
Pardalisca	His life isn't worth a penny! She says she wants to kill him! She's standing there, a sword –
Lysidamus	*What?*
Pardalisca	– a sword –
Lysidamus	What about the sword?
Pardalisca	– in her hand!
Lysidamus	Oh my god! What's she got *that* for?
Pardalisca	She's chasing everyone about the house and won't let anyone get near her! They're all hiding behind chests and under the beds, speechless with fear!
Lysidamus	(*aside*) Oh hell, that really puts paid to *everything*! (*Aloud*) What the blazes has got into the girl all of a sudden?
Pardalisca	She's out of her mind.
Lysidamus	I must be under some sort of curse! 1059
Pardalisca	If you only knew what she was saying just now!
Lysidamus	Well, what did she say? That's exactly what I want to know!
Pardalisca	She swore an oath by all the powers of heaven that she'd kill the man she slept beside tonight!
Lysidamus	(*without thinking*) Kill *me?*
Pardalisca	It's nothing to do with *you*, sir, is it?
Lysidamus	(*guiltily*) Oh, er, no.
Pardalisca	How are you mixed up with her?

Lysidamus	Er, I made a mistake – er, I meant to say 'the bailiff'.
Pardalisca	(*aside*) That was no mistake! You knew what you were saying, all right!
Lysidamus	But she's not threatening me *now*, is she?
Pardalisca	You're the very one she's angry with – you more than anyone!
Lysidamus	Why?
Pardalisca	Because you're marrying her to Olympio! She's determined not to let you *or* herself *or* her husband last the night! That's what I was sent out to tell you – to warn you to be on your guard against her! 1080
Lysidamus	Lord above us, I've had it now!
Pardalisca	(*aside*) Serves you right, too!
Lysidamus	(*aside*) I must be the unluckiest old man ever to have lived and loved!
Pardalisca	(*to audience*) I'm leading him *right* up the garden path! Everything I've told him is a pack of lies! My mistress and the next door neighbour here cooked the whole thing up between them, and they gave *me* the job of fooling him!
Lysidamus	Look, Pardalisca –
Pardalisca	What?
Lysidamus	There's something –
Pardalisca	What?
Lysidamus	There's something I want to ask you.
Pardalisca	(*pretending to go*) I'm in rather a hurry.
Lysidamus	And I'm in rather a mess! – Look, has Casina still got that sword?
Pardalisca	Yes! But it's not *one* sword – it's *two*!
Lysidamus	(*choking*) *Two?*
Pardalisca	She says she's going to do for you with one, and use the other on the bailiff! 1101
Lysidamus	(*aside*) I'm the deadest duck in existence! There's nothing for it – I'd better get dressed for battle! (*Aloud*) What about my wife, though? Didn't she try to take the sword away from her?
Pardalisca	Nobody dares go near her!
Lysidamus	Why doesn't she try persuasion?
Pardalisca	She is – but Casina says she'll only put her sword

145

down if she knows she's not going to be married to the bailiff.

Lysidamus   Well, she's going to marry him today whether she likes it or not. Just as a lesson. Why *shouldn't* my plan go through, why *shouldn't* she marry me – oops, my mistake, I meant the bailiff?

Pardalisca   You're making rather a lot of mistakes, aren't you, sir?

Lysidamus   Er – it's my tongue – I'm so scared, it's *paralysed*!... Look, tell my wife I'm *begging* her to get the girl to put the sword down and let me go back inside!   1120

Pardalisca   All right. I'll tell her.

Lysidamus   *You* plead with her, too!

Pardalisca   I'll plead with her, too.

Lysidamus   Use all the charm you've got – you know, the way you do! Listen – if you bring this off, I'll give you a pair of sandals and a gold ring for your finger, and all sorts of nice things.

Pardalisca   Leave it to me.

Lysidamus   Make sure you talk her round!

Pardalisca   I'm on my way – unless you've anything more to say?

Lysidamus   No – you go and see to it.

Pardalisca goes in. Lysidamus looks down the street.

Ah, here comes my trusty lieutenant at last, back from shopping. Look at that procession he's leading!

Olympio enters, followed by Citrio the cook, and assistants with foodstuffs.

Olympio   (*to Citrio*) Hey, Cook – watch it! Keep those thorns of yours in line! (*Gestures at the slaves*)

Citrio   What d'you mean, 'thorns'?   1138

Olympio   Well, everything they touch, they hang on to – but if you try to get it back they tear you to pieces! So wherever they go, wherever they are, they do double the normal damage to the people who hire them!

Citrio   Oh, come off it!

Olympio	(*seeing Lysidamus*) Aha! Now I'll put on a bit of style to go and meet my patron! (*Puts on a flowing cloak and swaggers about the stage*)
Lysidamus	My dear *fellow!*
Olympio	I am, yes. I can't deny it.
Lysidamus	Any news?
Olympio	You're in love: I'm hungry and thirsty. That's about it.

Olympio struts about, with Lysidamus following.

Lysidamus	(*flatteringly*) You're very elegantly turned out!
Olympio	(*keeping him at arm's length*) Aha, yes, today I'm really cutting a dash – no time for *your* sort!
Lysidamus	Hey, stand still for a moment! Don't be so snooty!
Olympio	Phew! *Phew!* What a stink your words put up!
Lysidamus	What's the matter?
Olympio	*This* (*points at Lysidamus*) is the matter.
Lysidamus	Won't you stand *still*?
Olympio	(*superciliously*) You really are being very *boring*, you know! 1161
Lysidamus	Look, if you don't stand still, I'll give you the mother and father of a hiding, and that's a promise! (*Grabs Olympio*)
Olympio	(*pulling away*) Lord – do keep away from me, can't you – you'll make me *heave*! (*Moves away*)
Lysidamus	Wait!
Olympio	Well? (*Stops, and turns slowly to look at Lysidamus*) Who *is* this fellow?
Lysidamus	Your master, that's who!
Olympio	Whose master?
Lysidamus	Yours – the one whose slave you are – remember?
Olympio	Me ... a slave?
Lysidamus	Yes. Mine.
Olympio	Aren't I free, then? (*Meaningfully*) Think hard! Think hard! (*Moving off again*)
Lysidamus	Wait! Stop! (*Grabs him again*)
Olympio	Let me alone.
Lysidamus	(*swallowing his pride*) It's *I* who am *your* slave, really.
Olympio	Oh, *that*'s better. 1179
Lysidamus	Please, Olympio, my dearest fellow, my own father,

147

my ... *patron* – I'm *begging* you!

Olympio Now you're talking.

Lysidamus I'm your man. It's true.

Olympio (*disdainfully*) What would *I* want with such a *rotten* slave?

Lysidamus *Well?* ... How soon do I get the kiss of life?

Olympio Oh, as soon as dinner's ready.

Lysidamus Have them (*gestures at Citrio and slaves*) go inside, then.

Olympio Off you go inside – hurry up and get dinner ready as soon as you can! I'll be right in. Mind you make it a really slap-up affair – something smart and elegant! I haven't got any time for that tasteless Roman rubbish! (*To Citrio*) Still there? Go on – get a move on! I'm staying here.
Citrio and slaves go inside.
(*To Lysidamus*) Nothing else, is there?

Lysidamus (*nodding at the house*) She says Casina's got a sword in there and she's going to use it – on both of us!

Olympio Oh, don't tell me! Let them get on with it! They're just being silly! They're a useless lot – I know them of old. Come on – you come along inside with me!

Lysidamus No. I'm scared of what might happen! You go in – take a look and see what's going on in there.   1203

Olympio Look, I value my skin as much as you do yours! But (*takes a deep breath*) just you go in! (*Pushes Lysidamus towards the door*)

Lysidamus All right, if you say so – I'll go (*grabs Olympio and holds him in front*) – but with you! Together!

Lysidamus and Olympio go in.

Some time has elapsed. Pardalisca enters, splitting her sides with laughter.

Pardalisca Lord, the Olympic Games were nothing like the fun and games we've had in there with old Lysidamus and his bailiff Olympio! Everyone's rushing about all over the house. The old boy's shouting in the kitchen, chivvying the cooks. 'Why don't you get on with it? Why don't you *produce* the meal, if

you're going to? Get a move on – dinner should
have been ready by now!' And the bailiff is walking
about with a garland on his head, all in white,
dressed to the nines! And the two ladies, well,
they're dressing up Chalinus the orderly, to give
him to our bailiff to marry in Casina's place! But
they're being very clever about it – pretending
they've no idea what's going to happen! And the
cooks are in it, too – it's really smart, the way
they're delaying the old boy's dinner – upsetting
pots, and pouring water over the fire – all this at
the request of the ladies, of course! What they want
is to drive the old boy out of the house without his
dinner, so they can stuff their own bellies to burst-
ing point! I know them all right, they're *colossal*
eaters: they can shift a whole shipload of supplies if
they get stuck in! (*Listens*) Wait! The door's
opening!   1231

Lysidamus comes out.

Lysidamus   (*to Cleostrata inside*) Well, dear, you two go ahead
and have dinner as soon as it's ready – that's the
best idea. I'll have mine at the farm. I thought I'd
accompany the bride and groom to the country –
well, I know what crooks there are about – just to
see no one tries to kidnap her. You enjoy your-
selves. But hurry up and send the happy couple out
here so we can get there while it's still light. I'll be
back tomorrow. I'll have my share of the dinner
then, dear.   1241

Pardalisca   (*aside*) Just as I predicted – the women are driving
the old boy out without his dinner!

Lysidamus   (*seeing her*) What are you doing here?

Pardalisca   I'm on an errand for my mistress, sir.

Lysidamus   Really?

Pardalisca   Yes, I promise.

Lysidamus   What are you snooping around here for?

Pardalisca   I'm *not* snooping around.

Lysidamus   On your way! (*Gestures at house*) While you're time-wasting here, the others have plenty to keep them busy.

Pardalisca I'm going. (*She moves off, but slowly*)

Lysidamus Well, off you go, then, you useless lump!

Pardalisca goes in. Lysidamus looks round.

Now I've got rid of her I can say what I like. Damn me, but if a man's in love, he can do without food even when he's *starving*!

The door opens.

Ah – here he comes, with garland and wedding torch – my ally, my comrade, my bailiff – my fellow-bridegroom!   1260

Olympio enters dressed as a bridegroom, all in white.

Olympio (*to musician*) Flautist! While they're bringing out the bride, make the whole street echo with a sweet song for my wedding! (*Singing, as a flautist strikes up*) 'Hymen, Hymen O Hymen O!'[6]

Lysidamus Well, how are you, my hero?

Olympio Hungry, that's how, and *not* feeling very heroic!

Lysidamus Well, *I*'m in love!

Olympio Well, I couldn't care less! You've got your love to keep you going – you don't need food! But my insides have been rumbling with emptiness for hours now!

Lysidamus Why are those women keeping us waiting so long in there, the slowcoaches? It seems almost as if it's deliberate! The more I hurry, the less progress they make!

Olympio Suppose I strike up the wedding song again and see if that brings them out any quicker?

Lysidamus Yes, a good idea. And seeing as I'm sharing this wedding with you, I'll give you a hand!

Olympio}
Lysidamus} 'Hymen, Hymen O Hymen O!'   1280

Lysidamus Hell, I'm having no luck at all! I could sing to Hymen till I popped – but still no chance of popping the way I want to!

Olympio By God, if you were a horse you'd be hard to handle!

150

Lysidamus	Why d'you say that?
Olympio	You've got a one-track mind!
Lysidamus	(*playfully making a move towards Olympio*) Sure it's only *one* track?
Olympio	(*horrified*) Ugh! Perish the thought! – Wait – there goes the door. They're coming out!
Lysidamus	Hooray! The gods are on my side after all!

The door opens. Pardalisca pops out and speaks.

Pardalisca	(*aside*) He's caught a distant whiff of Casinus already!

The wedding procession comes out: first Cleostrata, then Chalinus dressed as Casina, attended by maids.

Pardalisca	(*aloud*)

Gently, gently, o'er the threshold
Lift your footsteps, blushing bride!
Luck be with you on your journey,
But before you step inside:
Make a solemn resolution,
Enter marriage open-eyed!   1300

Master him and be the mistress,
Let your voice be loudly heard!
Be the one who gives the orders,
Always have the final word!

He must clothe you; you must fleece him,
Cheat your husband night and day!
Always practise to deceive him!
Now remember what I say!

Olympio	If she puts one foot out of place, she'll be very sorry indeed, I can tell you!
Lysidamus	Shh!
Olympio	I won't!
Lysidamus	What's the matter?
Olympio	It's that bitch Pardalisca – she's giving Casina all the wrong ideas!
Lysidamus	Look, are you trying to mess everything up when I've got it arranged so neatly? That's exactly what they want, that's precisely what they're after – to

	thwart everything we're trying to do!
Cleostrata	Come on, then, Olympio. Here she is. Take your bride, since you're so eager. 1321
Olympio	(*impatient*) Well, hand her over, then, if you're going to. (*Grabs Chalinus*)
Lysidamus	(*to Pardalisca and maids*) In you go!
Cleostrata	(*to Olympio*) Please, be *gentle* with her! She's a virgin – she's had no experience of men!
Olympio	Yes, yes.
Cleostrata	Goodbye!
Olympio	(*to the ladies*) You can go now.
Lysidamus	(*to the ladies*) Yes, off you go.
Cleostrata	Goodbye, then!

Cleostrata, Pardalisca and the maids go inside.

Lysidamus	(*looking round*) Has my wife gone?
Olympio	She's inside – relax!
Lysidamus	(*ecstatic*) Thank goodness! At last, at last I'm free! (*To Chalinus*) Oh, my little sweetheart! My little darling! My pretty little breath of springtime!
Olympio	Hey, watch it, you, or I'll clock you one! The girl's mine!
Lysidamus	I know – but I get first bite of the cherry!
Olympio	Hold this torch. 1340
Lysidamus	(*throwing an arm round Chalinus*) No. I'd rather hold *this*! (*Ecstatic*) Oh Venus, Venus the omnipotent, what a prize you gave me when you made this young girl mine!
Olympio	(*also embracing Chalinus*) Oh, darling wife – the softness of your body! – Ow! What was *that* for?
Lysidamus	What's the matter?
Olympio	She stood on my foot – it felt like an *elephant*!
Lysidamus	Sh! be quiet! (*Caressing Chalinus*) Her breast – it's softer than a cloud!
Olympio	(*trying again*) Ah, what a *pretty* little rosebud – ouch! *Ouch!*
Lysidamus	What is it?
Olympio	That was no *elbow* she dug in my chest – it felt like a *battering-ram*!
Lysidamus	Well, for heaven's sake, why are you so rough with

	her? *I* do it nice and gently, and she doesn't cut up rough with me! – *Ow!*
Olympio	What's up? 1359
Lysidamus	Well! What a powerful little thing she is! She just nudged me, and she nearly laid me flat on my back!
Olympio	(*sniggering*) She must be hinting it's bedtime!
Lysidamus	Well, why don't we go, then?
Olympio	(*to the bride*) Trip along, you pretty, pretty little dear!

Olympio steers her towards Alcesimus's house. The three go in.

Some time has passed. Cleostrata, Myrrhina and Pardalisca re-enter.

Myrrhina	That was a really splendid dinner we had – and now we've come outside to see the wedding-games! Dear me, I've never laughed so much in all my life – I don't think I'll ever laugh so much again, either!
Pardalisca	I'd *love* to know what Chalinus is doing now – the blushing bridegroom with his blushing – husband!
Myrrhina	This plot of ours, it was a real *masterpiece* – I don't know any playwright who dreamed up a better one!
Cleostrata	How I'd love to see the old fool coming out now with a couple of black eyes! Really, he must be the filthiest old goat alive – (*to Myrrhina*) unless we award that title to the man who lent him his home? Now Pardalisca, I want you to stand guard so that you can poke fun at whoever comes out first.
Pardalisca	I will, with *pleasure*! You know me! 1381
Cleostrata	(*places Pardalisca in doorway*) You stand here and keep your eyes open, and tell us what they're up to inside. Behind me, there's a good girl.
Myrrhina	Yes – then you'll be able to say just what you want to.
Cleostrata	Sh! That was your door I heard!

The three women withdraw into Cleostrata's doorway. Olympio comes out, much the worse for wear.

Olympio	Where can I run? Where can I hide? I'll *never* live this down, never! My god, we're really in disgrace now, my master and I, with this 'marriage' of ours! The *shame* of it! And the fright I've had! And we're both a laughing stock now! (*Thinking*) Oh dear! What an idiot I've been! Ashamed! That's a new feeling for me: I've never been *that* before! (*To audience*) Here, listen now, while I tell you what happened – I promise you it's worth your trouble; my escapade in there makes pretty funny listening – *and* telling! 1398
	When I'd got my bride inside, I took her straight to a bedroom – it was dark as a dungeon in there! 'You lie down, dear,' I says to her – this was before the old boy had arrived. Well, I saw she was comfy, I propped her up on some cushions, put her at her ease, and whispered sweet nothings in her ear – well, I wanted to get her wedded and bedded before the old man had arrived, see? But I began really slowly – I didn't want to rush things; still, I kept on having to look over my shoulder in case the old man was around. First, just to get her in the mood, I asked her for a long, lingering kiss. She pushed my hand away and wouldn't let me kiss her! Well, by now I was in more of a hurry – by this time I felt like throwing myself on her – I wanted to steal a march on old Lysidamus, so I bolted the door in case he came in and caught me at it.
Cleostrata	(*aside to Pardalisca*) Go on – now! Go up to him!
Pardalisca	(*Stepping from doorway, to Olympio*) Where's the bride, then, eh?
Olympio	(*aside*) Oh my god! The cat's out of the bag!
Pardalisca	(*overhearing*) Well, then – you'd better tell me exactly what happened. What's going on inside there? 1422
Olympio	(*uncomfortably*) I .. can't tell you!
Pardalisca	Come on – you began – now carry on.
Olympio	I'm ... ashamed to!
Pardalisca	Don't be so feeble! After you got into bed, what happened *then*? Start from there!

Olympio	It's *shame*ful, that's what it is!
Pardalisca	Well, it'll be a lesson to those that listen, then.
Olympio	It's preposterous, really!
Pardalisca	You're wasting time. Go on!
Olympio	Well .. when I felt down ... underneath her –
Pardalisca	What?
Olympio	Unbelievable!
Pardalisca	*What?*
Olympio	Incredible!
Pardalisca	Well, what *was* it?

1438

Olympio	It was *enormous*, that's what it was! I thought she'd got a sword, so I began to feel about her for it; then, while I was looking for the sword, I grabbed hold of the handle to something – but there was no sword attached! On second thoughts, the handle would have been cold, anyway!
Pardalisca	Go on!
Olympio	I ... don't *like* to!
Pardalisca	(*bubbling over with laughter*) Was it – a horseradish, perhaps?
Olympio	No!
Pardalisca	A cucumber?
Olympio	*That* was no vegetable, I tell you – well, if it was, it would have won all the first prizes! Whatever it was, it was a giant variety – king-size!
Pardalisca	What happened then? Go on!

1454

Olympio	Then I tried to win her round by chatting to her. 'Casina, dear, *please*,' I says, 'you're my dear little wife now; why are you so unkind to your husband, eh? This really isn't very fair; I don't deserve such treatment, just because I *wanted* you so badly!' She didn't say a word – all she did was to pull at her dress and cover her ... well, what *you*'ve got that I haven't! Well, when I see *that* road blocked, I ask her if I can – er – try the other. So, to turn her over, I put my arms round her waist – still not so much as a word from her – but I couldn't budge her – she was strong as a horse! So I got up – er – to see ... to try something else ... *you* know!

155

Myrrhina   (*to Cleostrata, aside*) I wouldn't have missed *this* for *anything*!

Olympio   (*continuing*) Well ... I bent down to give her a kiss, and what happens? My lips get pricked by a beard as tough as a scrubbing brush! Then – I'm kneeling over her – she lifts up both her feet and bashes away at my chest! I fell right off the bed flat on my face, and she jumps up and starts hammering away at my head! Well, that was enough. I made a dash for the door without saying another word – that's why I'm in *this* mess – ! I thought the old man could get a taste of the same medicine – and serve him right!   1480

Pardalisca   (*aside*) Couldn't be better! (*To Olympio*) But where's your cloak?

Olympio   I left it in there. (*Points*)

Pardalisca   Well, now – you've been properly had, both of you, wouldn't you say?

Olympio   (*shamefaced*) Yes – and no more than we deserved. (*Alarmed*) Listen! That was the door! She's not still after me, is she?

Lysidamus enters, also in a terrible state.

Lysidamus   Oh, the *disgrace* of it – the ghastly, awful *disgrace* of it! *What* on earth can I do in a mess like *this*? How can I look my wife in the face? I don't know! This is the end of me – I'm *finished*! It's all out now – the whole wretched business! I've had it – there's no way out! They've really got me over a barrel – caught red-handed! There's no possible excuse I can give my wife – look at me – what a picture! In tatters, and my staff and cloak gone, too! Well, so much for my secret romance – I suppose I'd better go and take what's coming to me. I'll go in and crawl to her – I'll offer my back for compensation! (*To audience*) Is there anyone out there who'd like to change places with me? I've no *idea* what to do now – unless it's what no-good slaves do – I mean do a bunk! If I go back home, I'll be flayed alive!... Eh? Think I'm talking nonsense, do you? Well, I don't like getting knocked about, even if I *have* deserved it! I'll go ... *that* way, I think – and quickly!

Lysidamus sets out past Alcesimus's house – as Chalinus emerges from it. Chalinus is carrying Lysidamus's staff and cloak.

Chalinus	Hey! Stop right where you are, you old goat! 1508
Lysidamus	Oh my god! Someone's calling me back. I'll pretend I didn't hear. (*Continuing to run away*)
Chalinus	Come on, let's be having you – yes, *you*, that's right, the one who thinks he can carry on like some Massilian nancy-boy! Now's your chance, if you want to have a crack at me. Come on back to the bedroom, if you want to! (*Changing tone*) This is your comeuppance! Come on – just step this way! I've got a sure-fire way of settling things (*taps Lysidamus's staff meaningfully*) without going to court!
Lysidamus	(*aside*) Help! This fellow's dead set on defluffing me where it hurts! I'll have to go *this* way (*turns suddenly past his own house*); *that* way I'll be crippled for life!
Cleostrata	(*blocking his path*) Hullo, Ladykiller! 1522
Lysidamus	(*aside*) Oh, no – my wife – no escaping her, either! ... Now I'm between the devil and the deep blue sea – I don't know *which* way to run! Wolves on one side, dogs on the other! And the wolf is wielding a stick, too! Help! I think I'll give the lie to the old proverb – I'll go *this* way and just hope the dog omen is luckier![7]
Myrrhina	What are you up to, you *bigamist*!
Cleostrata	Where can my husband have come from looking like *this*? (*To Lysidamus*) What happened to the stick you had, and the cloak you were wearing?
Myrrhina	He lost them when he was up to his dirty business with Casina, *I* bet.
Lysidamus	(*croaking*) This is my lot!
Chalinus	(*teasing*) Let's go to bed again, shall we? (*Putting on a high voice*) It's me! *Casina!*
Lysidamus	Oh, go to hell!
Chalinus	Don't you love me any more? 1540
Cleostrata	Go on, tell me: what happened to your cloak?

Lysidamus	(*frantically searching for an excuse*) Er – it was ... er ... some Bacchic revellers, dear, yes, I swear –
Cleostrata	(*incredulous*) Bacchic revellers?
Lysidamus	Yes ... I swear, dear –
Myrrhina	He's talking rubbish, and he knows it. Everybody knows there aren't any Bacchic revels any more.[8]
Lysidamus	Oh, no, I forgot!... Well, but anyway, some Bacchic revellers –
Cleostrata	What do you mean, Bacchic revellers?
Lysidamus	(*miserably*) ... well, if that's impossible –
Cleostrata	Lord, look at the state you're in!
Lysidamus	Me?
Cleostrata	Yes – you're telling a pack of lies! Look how pale you've gone! Aren't you *ashamed* of yourself?
Lysidamus	Why ... why should I lie to you? 1556
Cleostrata	You want me to spell it out? You and your dirty philandering! An old man of your years, too! What an escapade! Well, you really have distinguished yourself, and no mistake! Congratulations! But we caught you out – by enlisting the aid of (*points at Chalinus*) – Casinus here! *Now* are you going to confess?
Olympio	It was all his fault, ma'am – him and his dirty ways. He was the one who made me turn to wickedness!
Lysidamus	(*aside*) Can't you keep your mouth shut?
Olympio	(*aloud*) No, I won't keep my mouth shut! It was your fault – you kept on and on, begging me to ask to marry Casina – just because you fancied her yourself!
Lysidamus	(*acutely embarrassed*) Er – I did *that*?
Olympio	(*sarcastically*) No, it was Hector of Troy!
Lysidamus	He'd have stuffed you for a start, then! (*To the ladies*) Er – did I *really* do what you say?
Cleostrata	I don't know how you have the nerve to keep asking!
Lysidamus	Well, then, if I did ... it was very wrong of me.
Cleostrata	Just you go back inside! I'll remind you all right if your memory's a little vague! 1580
Lysidamus	(*uneasily*) Er – I'd rather take your word for it, I

think! (*Abjectly*) My dear, please forgive your husband just this once! Myrrhina, do ask her to, please! And if ever I make love to Casina again – or even look as if I might – let alone actually making love to her – if I ever misbehave myself like this again, my dear – you can hang, draw and quarter me! And you'd have every right!

Myrrhina (*to Cleostrata*) I really think you might forgive him just this once, Cleostrata!

Cleostrata All right, if you say so. (*To Lysidamus*) And I'm forgiving you without more ado for one reason only: this play's already gone on long enough, and I suggest we don't make it any longer!

Lysidamus (*overjoyed*) You're not angry?

Cleostrata No, I'm not angry.

Lysidamus May I take your word for that?

Cleostrata You may.

Lysidamus No man on earth can have a sweeter wife than I have! 1600

Cleostrata (*to Chalinus*) Now give him back his stick and cloak.

Chalinus (*handing them over reluctantly*) All right, have 'em, if you want. But I tell you, it's a dead diabolical liberty the way I've been treated! I married two men – and neither of them did his stuff on his wedding night!

Chalinus steps forward and delivers the Epilogue.

Friends, in case you're wondering, we'll tell you what's going to happen inside (*gestures at the house*): Casina turns out to be the daughter of the gentleman who lives next door, and marries Euthynicus, our young master! *That*'s what!

Now it's time for you to give a deserving cast the sort of applause it deserves! (*Confidentially*) Those who do will always have as much fun on the side as they want – and the wife'll be none the wiser!...
But those who don't clap us loud and long, look out! – or you'll find yourself sharing a bed with a ... billy goat bathed in bilge-water!

159

NOTES TO CASINA

1 A pun on the name Plautus, which apparently could mean a dog with soft, flapping ears.
2 Drawing lots was a common way of settling disputes, both in private and public life.
3 The marked lots were drawn from an urn filled with water, the water being presumably to prevent the marks being visible. The lots were made of pebbles or some hard wood which did not float.
4 Cresphontes and the sons of Aristodemus drew lots over the division of the Peloponnese. One lot was of sun-dried clay, the other of clay baked by fire. The former dissolved in the water; the latter, being properly baked, came out first.
5 The text is uncertain, but the Latin words are supposed to sound like the blackbird's song.
6 'Hymen, Hymen O Hymen O!' was a ritual cry raised at weddings, which originally apparently had no specific meaning; the belief in a marriage god Hymen was a derivation from the wedding song.
7 The old proverb referred to was: 'There's no safety between wolves and dogs' – something like our saying 'between the devil and the deep blue sea'.
8 In 186 B.C. the Senate finally banned the worship of Bacchus because the rites had acquired a notoriety for sexual irregularity and other disorders.